LOOK UP

Your Unexpected Guide to Good

Jan Sokoloff Harness

creativeinstigation.com

Published in the United States by Running Duck Press,
an imaginary division of Sokoloff Harness Communications LLC

ISBN: 978-0-578-54329-1
FIRST EDITION

Cover and text design by Joann Bittel

"The world is violent and mercurial—it will have its way with you.
We are saved only by love—love for each other and the love that we pour
into the art we feel compelled to share: being a parent; being a writer; being
a painter; being a friend. We live in a perpetually burning building, and
what we must save from it, all the time, is love."

— *Tennessee Williams*

TABLE OF CONTENTS

LOOK UP?

Somewhere in this book—you'll find it—there's a moment where I talk about writing book titles in my head. I come up with great titles for nonexistent books all the time. *Flying Fish and Other Fancies*, for example. And yet, when it came time to name this book, I floundered.

The first title was *Hineni*, a great Hebrew word that means, "Here I am."
As in, fully present. As in, paying attention. As in, completely focused on
you. Can you remember the last time you held someone's full attention?
WHAT A GIFT.

The meaning of "hineni" is lovely, but the word itself means
absolutely nothing to 99.9 percent of the universe. Heck, I read Hebrew
and I can't even pronounce it correctly. **SO. NO.**

The next title was *Creative Instigation*, also a perfectly fine
idea. After all, the book is largely culled from nearly 1,300 posts on the
Creative Instigation blog, an online adventure I launched in 2007.
If you're looking for all 1,300 posts, God bless you real good and visit
CREATIVEINSTIGATION.COM.

Creative Instigation was a logical choice, and yet ... the book is
about a lot more than creativity. Plus, the very word "creative" distracts
people. Whenever I do a presentation on writing or creativity, I can
guarantee that someone will come up and apologetically tell me, "I don't
have a creative bone in my body." If you have ever said—or thought—
anything remotely like that, I have immediate advice for you. Stop reading
this introduction. Flip to the quiz on the next page. Take the quiz. You are
far more creative than you realize, and I can prove it.

But, back to the business at hand. How did I land on *Look Up*?
The title fell into place one day when I was thinking about Lillian Sokoloff,
my mom, mentor, and muse. Since she's not with us on earth anymore,
I did what I naturally do when I think of her.

I LOOKED UP.

When my brother and sister and I were kids, Mom created fun days. A fun
day was what people call a staycation now—we'd start with breakfast out,

/2/

go to a movie or shopping or bowling, eat lunch, go to the Kansas City Zoo or the Nelson Art Gallery, and not come home until evening.

Fun days were fabulous. While I can't remember all that we did, one moment in downtown Kansas City stands out. We were walking by Kline's department store, and I was concerned about the metal vents in the sidewalk. I was 8 years old. Falling into the sidewalk abyss, into what was undoubtedly a dungeon, felt like a real and present danger. This, I thought, was not fun.

Fortunately, while I obsessed on the perilous pavement, Mom focused on happy.

"Look up!" she prodded me. "Look up! Look at those buildings! Do you see those carvings? Those are gargoyles. Have you ever seen anything like them?"

I had not. And those huge stone gargoyles were so cool, I forgot to be afraid. I walked right over the sidewalk slats and lived to tell the tale.

/3/

FACT IS,
I LIVED TO TELL A LOT OF TALES.

Look Up: Your Unexpected Guide to Good gives me the chance to share a few tales with you, as we turn down the discord that surrounds us, and turn up the volume on all the beauty and joy and kindness that's still out there.

With Lillian as our virtual guide, *Look Up* takes us on a collaborative creative journey. I hope you find something in this book that makes you laugh. Something that makes you cry. Something that makes you think. Possibly at the same time. Most of all, I hope *Look Up* reminds you that no matter how non-creative, isolated, or weird you may sometimes think you are, you are not alone.

Look Up, my friend. Look around. It's a beautiful world, and we are all in this together.

your CREATIVITY QUIZ

Are you creative? Let's find out ...

1. Are you choosing your own clothes today?

   ☐ YES   ☐ NO   ☐ MAYBE

2. Have you ever made someone who was sad feel better?

   ☐ YES   ☐ NO   ☐ MAYBE

3. Can you write a sentence that conveys exactly what you want?

   ☐ YES   ☐ NO   ☐ MAYBE

4. Can you cook anything without a recipe?

   ☐ YES   ☐ NO   ☐ MAYBE

   Do you vary the spices now and then?

   ☐ YES   ☐ NO   ☐ MAYBE

5. Can you paint, knit, dance, quilt, or play the flute?

   ☐ YES   ☐ NO   ☐ MAYBE

   Can you play any musical instrument?

   ☐ YES   ☐ NO   ☐ MAYBE

6. Do you know how to tune an engine?

   ☐ YES   ☐ NO   ☐ MAYBE

7. If you had the right tools and material, could you build a deck?

☐ **YES** ☐ **NO** ☐ **MAYBE**

8. Have you ever suggested an idea in a business meeting?

☐ **YES** ☐ **NO** ☐ **MAYBE**

9. Can you program a computer?

☐ **YES** ☐ **NO** ☐ **MAYBE**

/5/

10. If you miss a highway exit, do you give up and park on the shoulder?

Or, do you find another way home?

☐ **YES** ☐ **NO** ☐ **MAYBE**

You may have answered all those questions with, "Jan, you're buggin'."
I've heard it before. Heck, I'm thinking of putting UR BUGN on my VW's
license plate. But here's the simple fact:

WE ARE ALL CREATIVE.
AND THAT INCLUDES YOU.

If you answered even one question with a "Yes," mazel tov! You get a gold star for creativity. FYI, questions #3 and #5 are no more important than the others. You may not be a painter or a poet or a photographer. Some of us have talents—and work hard to hone them—in areas other people lack.

Isn't that wonderful?

We're not all the same. But we are all creative. We all see possibilities and problems, and create new answers and solutions.

Best of all,

the possibility exists,

every day,

to reinvent ourselves,

and

—as we do—

make the world better in that creative process.

CHAPTER ONE:

LESSONS FROM MY MOTHER

MAY YOU LIVE LIKE LILLIAN

When I began work on this book, my mom was alive. Today, she is not. And yet ...

Lillian Marie Sokoloff is always with me. I know her goodness, laughter, and light made a lasting impression on many others too— including those who read the *Creative Instigation* blog over the years. Mom inspired dozens of posts, and her posts always generated comments.

When Mom passed away on Nov. 25, 2018, our family was immediately surrounded by love and kind words.

"That firecracker of a mom of yours certainly will be missed, by her family, but also by the world that was exposed to her **UNBRIDLED JOY**."

"Lil was such a **JOYFUL LIGHT** in this world."

"I'm so sorry your mom is gone, but grateful **HER LEGACY OF FINDING GOOD AND JOY IN EVERYTHING AND EVERYONE LIVES ON** through her family."

THE RECURRING THEME? JOY.

Mom did find good and joy in everything and everyone. She was a creative wonder, capable of turning everyday moments into special events. She never lost her spark. During her last year, there were times I thought we'd get thrown out of bingo for excessive giggling.

/8/

I have trouble talking about Mom in past tense, so let me say: My mother is a blessing. May we learn from Lillian.

Posted on Feb. 3, 2009

THE **FLOWER LADY**

NO MATTER WHAT OUR TALENTS ARE, WE CAN **ALL CREATE MORE HAPPINESS** IN THE WORLD.

I was reminded of this when my sister Eva and I went to Mom's apartment to reorganize her clothes. Even at 87, Mom is fun and fabulous—something it's easy to forget while cleaning closets.

While Eva and I were sorting clothes, Diana came to visit. Diana used to work at Village Shalom, the retirement community where Mom lives, and she and Mom bonded over a love of laughter and daisies. When she left her job, Diana promised to come back once a month to visit and bring flowers.

/9/

You know what's amazing? She's doing it. This wonderful woman, who has a family of her own and a more-than-full schedule, shows up on the first Sunday of every month. She spends an hour or so chatting with Mom. She brings a bouquet. She brings joy. Mom is thrilled that Diana cares about her, and takes huge delight in looking at, and bragging about, her flowers.

One hour. Once a month. Twelve hours a year. It's a small investment of time with a huge and happy payoff.

UPDATE: As Mom got older and her memory got weaker, we referred to Diana as the flower lady. Diana continued to bring flowers, on the first Sunday of the month, until Mom passed away. Every month. For years. And, knowing that Mom loved sweets too, Diana's husband always sent baked goods. As a final tribute, they brought a bouquet and brownies to Mom's memorial service. If you ever doubt the goodness of the universe, remember this.

Posted on Nov. 4, 2009

RUN with ME

When I was a kid, my family drove to California on vacation. I had never seen the ocean before, so this was a huge deal to me. By the time we got to the beach, I was jumping-up-and-down excited.

It was the most wonderful, magical, marvelous thing I had ever seen.

Being a kid, I wanted to run right into the waves, fully dressed. Being a good kid, I didn't. I asked Mom for permission.

/10/ Now, Mom could have responded to my enthusiasm by reminding me that I wasn't wearing a swimsuit, I'd ruin my clothes, and I needed to have a little patience. She could have said, "Sure, honey, go on in." She didn't do either of those. Instead, Mom took my hand and ran into the waves with me.

WHEN SOMEONE APPROACHES YOU

with PURE ENTHUSIASM FOR AN IDEA,

A POSSIBILITY,

A HALF-BAKED THOUGHT,

WHAT'S YOUR RESPONSE?

Do you squash the energy with logic? Do you encourage them to take their concept to the next level? Or do you grab hold of their enthusiasm and run with it?

TODAY, LET'S RUN.

Posted on March 3, 2010

YOUR WORK MATTERS

My first job was at Putsch's Cafeteria at Ward Parkway Shopping Center in Kansas City. I was 15 years old, and it was not my dream job. I wrapped silverware. Every Saturday, 9-5. That's a heckuva lot of utensils.

Mom would periodically come to Putsch's to eat lunch with me. She'd take a silverware bundle out of the bin at the start of the line, hold it up like a trophy, and proudly announce to everyone within hearing distance, **"NO ONE WRAPS IT LIKE YOU DO, JANET!"**

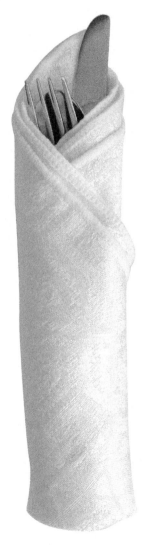

/11/

Silly? Sure. Important? You bet. While I might groan and roll my eyes, I went back to work ready to wrap. And I rolled those napkins tight. Because even if it didn't matter to everyone, it mattered to Mom.

Whether we're at work or at home, what we say to each other makes a difference. What we do for each other matters. Don't just do your job. Do it right.

FULL DISCLOSURE:

I worked at Putsch's 39 years ago. Mom still thinks I wrap silverware better than anyone.

Posted on April 23, 2015

MY FAVORITE **POET**

Those of you who know me well might guess that my favorite poet is E. E. Cummings. Or Robert Frost. Perhaps Dorothy Parker? I love 'em all. But none of them compare with my first and favorite poet: Lillian Sokoloff.

Let me tell you a story about Mom, who celebrates her 94th birthday today. When she was a young woman, she was offered a job writing greeting cards for Hallmark.

JANET: Why didn't you take the job, Mom?

MOM: I didn't want to write for them, Janet. They had too many rules.

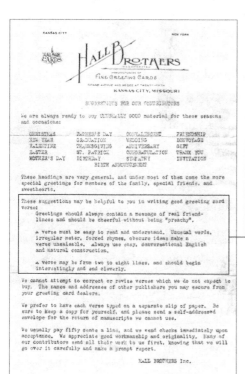

THE RULES

Greetings should always contain a message of real friendliness and should be cheerful without being "preachy".

A verse must be easy to read and understand. Unusual words, irregular meter, forced rhymes, obscure ideas make a verse unsaleable. Always use easy, conversational English and natural construction.

A verse may be from two to eight lines, and should begin interestingly and end cleverly.

God bless her.

Here's a poem from Mom that has been published in several magazines and in *The Kansas City Star*. She wrote it according to her own rules and, to my knowledge, never gave it a title:

/13/

> Too quick are we to criticize,
>
> Too slow are we to praise,
>
> The comings and the goings
>
> Of other people's ways.

> If only we would stop to think
>
> Before the words come out,
>
> Perhaps a nicer thought would come
>
> For us to talk about.

> So next time you are tempted,
>
> Unkind things you are about to say,
>
> Stop, reflect, remember,
>
> What you have read today.

> — *Lillian Marie Sokoloff*

**YOU CATCH MORE FLIES WITH HONEY
THAN YOU DO WITH VINEGAR.**

Posted on Oct. 29, 2015

CHANGE IS SCARY

For decades ... decades ... we've had Mom out to our house for Halloween. The tradition is simple and dear: Tom, my husband, makes his world-famous taco soup; we have dinner; then I get Mom set up at the front door, where she hands out candy to all the adorable trick-or-treaters.

During the past few years, I've been impressed with how well behaved the kids are, as they patiently wait for Mom to ooh and ahh over their costumes, and then try to drop the candy into their buckets. Her macular degeneration is at the point now where she can't see the buckets. (I'm not sure she can see the costumes either, but she certainly acts like she can.)

/15/

ONE MOTHER TOLD ME THAT HER CHILDREN ALWAYS LOOK FORWARD TO GOING TO THE HOUSE WITH THE NICE OLD LADY.

This year, the nice old lady won't be there. I've decided she's not up to it. Mom turned 94 in April and the past year has been a difficult one. She rarely stays up past 7 p.m. Unusual activities exhaust her. Her memory is no longer linear. One day she'll know me and everything about me. The next day, she'll wonder if I'm her sister.

She can't remember ever being at my house. I haven't had the heart to ask if she remembers Halloween.

So, this year, I'll be at the door and I'll do my best to live up to Mom's example. I'll ooh and ahh and hand out the treats. I know some of the kids will be disappointed that the nice old lady isn't there. I hope they have no idea how disappointed I am.

THE FLOWERS IN HER FIELD OF VISION

Our mother can't see

The flowers my brother brought

No matter where I move the vase.

But, as I hold them way off to the left,

She pretends she can see them, with oohs and aahs,

And I pretend to believe her, as we both agree:

There's no scent sweeter than fresh-cut roses,

Hand-delivered by my brother.

Posted on Dec. 11, 2015

YOU GOTTA LAUGH

I hardly ever tell jokes, because I can't remember them. One of the few I can remember is:

> *"What's the difference between a Jewish mother and a vulture?"*
> *"A vulture waits until you're dead to eat your heart out."*

I always thought that was funny. Lillian still doesn't agree.

But here's one even Mom would like—although she never curses and this does have an obscenity in it:

> *A man takes his family to the zoo. When they get there, much to their surprise, they discover the zoo only has one animal—a dog! And the man turns to his family and says, "It's a shih tzu."*

Ha! Makes me laugh every time.

/17/

UPDATE: Honest to Pete, I'm not making it up: Mom never said a cuss word her entire life. Never. Not one. She loved words and thought using vulgarity was a sure sign that you weren't smart enough, or trying hard enough, to find the right word to express your feelings. I inherited her love of words. Unfortunately, I sometimes feel that **DAMNITALLTOHELL** is exactly the right word.

THOSE CUSS WORDS THAT BEGIN WITH "D"
I NEVER USE - OH NO! NOT ME!

A HAPPY BIRTHDAY
WITH ONE
HELOFALOT
OF D___
FINE JOYS
Feb. 12, 1939
40 yrs. old
Sunday That hit the spot!
With loads of love to
My adorable Mother
from Daughter Lillian.

Posted on Sept. 19, 2016

IT'S NOT OK to CRY

After reading yet another Facebook post from a friend in crisis, I've decided that T. S. Eliot is wrong.

APRIL IS NOT THE CRUELEST MONTH.
SEPTEMBER IS.

So, here in the midst of September, we all need this reminder: *It's not OK to cry.*

Now, if tears were flames, I burst into spontaneous combustion at least 10 times last Tuesday. Don't worry; there's nothing horrible going on. It wasn't a crisis. It was the sucker punch of life, the combination of countless hurts and frustrations and losses and irritations and worries and failures, those moments we push down and ignore so we can make it through the day.

On Tuesday, I went to Village Shalom, Mom's assisted living complex. I gave flowers to the wonderful nurse who has taken such good care of Mom and is leaving to go back to school. I told Mom who I was, something I do repeatedly these days.

Then I went out to the parking lot, got into my car, sat there, and sobbed. And I continued to burst into spontaneous tears throughout the day.

You know what happened? I woke up Wednesday and felt lighter. I felt happier. I felt like myself again. And that's when I remembered ...

It's not OK to cry. It's essential. It's life-affirming. It's cleansing. Crying is visceral proof that we are feeling, caring, emotional beings. Crying is human.

And I rarely do it, because I'm pretty damn busy being strong and stoic, when I ought to **JUST BE.**

If you, like far too many of my friends, are going through a tough day, month, year, here's my advice: Find a sanctuary. Maybe it's your home. Your car. A quiet stretch on a familiar path. Then, if you need to cry, let the waterfall flow.

I often find sanctuary in solitude. You may prefer to cry on someone's shoulder. Either way, when hearts are heavy and eyes are full, we are not alone. Ancient sages are right beside us, quietly whispering:

"THIS TOO SHALL PASS."

Posted on Oct. 24, 2016

ARE YOU WARM ENOUGH?

Last Thursday night, Mom fell—a common occurrence these days—but this time she broke her wrist. The ambulance took her to St. Luke's South hospital, I met her at the ER, and we spent several hours with a truly wonderful healthcare team. A few X-rays and sedatives later, her wrist was set, and they helped me settle her in the car for the quick drive back home to Village Shalom.

By this time, it was around midnight and the temperature had dropped to about 45 degrees. It was chilly, and Mom was wearing a cotton nightie. We tucked a blanket around her legs. As luck would have it, I had one of her jackets in the car, so I wrapped that around her shoulders.

Keep this in mind: Mom is 95, in pain, confused, and cold. And you know what she asked as I drove her home?

"Are you warm enough, Janet?"

One of the keys to living a long and happy life is caring about others. Even with her skittish memory, Mom never forgets to ask about me and my family and to wish us well. She never forgets that other people matter. And that extends to people she doesn't know: At the hospital, Mom repeatedly expressed her gratitude to the doctor and nurses and X-ray technicians—and asked questions about them.

I told her, as we drove, that she had been an excellent patient.

"I try to be as good as I can, Janet. That's just how I was raised."

Lillian Sokoloff raises the bar daily for what it means to be a good person. Her concern for me, our family, the people around us? Well, that's enough to comfort me, no matter how cold this world might seem.

UPDATE: This happened two years before Mom died, yet when the ER doctor heard the news, she felt moved to send us a condolence card. Her message read, in part, "In that one brief visit to the Emergency Department, your mom made an impact on me. She was so sweet and delightful."

EVERY MOMENT OF KINDNESS MATTERS, DEAR HEART.
EVERY MOMENT MATTERS.

Posted on Nov. 16, 2016

WHAT ARE **YOU** WAITING FOR?

Mom recently had the delight of a visit with the Nelson family. Christie and OJ and their daughters, Libby and Laura, no longer live in Kansas City, but they came back—and one of the big reasons why was to see Mom.

Their connection goes back 29 years; Mom babysat for both girls. The visit was pure joy for everyone—Mom's room was filled with laughter and love and happy memories.

Mom is getting on in years. Time is precious. But you know what? Time is precious for all of us, regardless of our age.

/22/   How are you spending your time today? **WHO** should you visit? **WHO** should you call? What should you create?

And what are you waiting for?

Is who right? Or should it be whom? Oy.

UPDATE : Yep. Even writers forget the rules. But I won't keep you dangling: According to Teena, my personal grammar guru, "whom" would be the correct choice technically (if we were being old school), but it's ok for me to use "who" as an interrogative here, because it fits my style.

Posted on April 23, 2018

THE PIP AT THE PARTY

One of the most creative forces in the universe turns 97 today. When the family gathered to celebrate Mom's birthday, she sang songs, laughed, ate pizza and cupcakes, and said the flavored LaCroix was "the best water I ever had—it really has some pip!"

Mom really has some pip.

Today, in honor of her birthday, I'm sharing a couple of the "secrets" that keep her young and creative:

1. **MOM IS ALWAYS WILLING TO BE DELIGHTED.** Think about that. She approaches all activities—from a meal to a bingo game—expecting good things. It's not optimism. It's faith. Mom has a rock-solid faith that everything happens for the best.

2. **MOM IS OBSERVANT.** When she was younger and we'd go out together, Mom was always encouraging us to, "Look up!" Sometimes, there were gargoyles, perfectly perched on buildings. Sometimes, there were clouds that looked like ... well, you had to tell her. "What does that cloud look like to you?" There was no wrong answer.

3. **MOM IS GRATEFUL.** There are some incredibly grumpy people in her nursing home. She's not one of them. She still thanks the people who help her, and asks them questions. She's still engaged in their lives and grateful for their assistance.

I could go on, but three is magical—as is Mom. Help me celebrate her today:

Be delighted. Look up, and find something & someone to be grateful for!

/23/

LIVE LIKE LILLIAN

Every year, no matter how infrequently I post on the *Creative Instigation* blog, I try to wrap things up with a New Year's wish for all the readers who have stuck with me and my random postings. This year is no different.

This year is completely different.

I am very sorry to share the news that my mother passed away on Sunday, Nov. 25. Ordinarily, I would use "died" rather than "passed away," but Mom truly just slipped away. Her passing can only be described as a good death: She was 97 years old; she had seen all three of her children in the week before she went; she wasn't ill or in pain; she was at home and surrounded by love; she was up and ready for the day; she closed her eyes and peacefully passed.

The last words she said to me and my siblings were, "I love you."

I'll write more about Mom in the days ahead, but for now, I want to give you this:

May you have faith. May you wake every day eager to see what happens next. May you be willing to be delighted. May you look for the best in everyone and everything. May you face challenges with courage and strength. May you write poetry. May you play bingo or mah jongg or a board game with people you love. May you celebrate every win. May you forgive and forget. May you always be a flirt. May you create a family of friends. May you live a life that helps and cheers and inspires others. May you live like Lillian.

CHAPTER TWO:

IMAGINATION IN ACTION
ANOTHER LOOK AT YOU

Mom wasn't online to read my *Creative Instigation* blog, but she was tickled that posts about her were always reader favorites. The blog and this book are my response to a universal wall of denial, one I run up against all the time. I could be talking about writing or landscaping or decorating cupcakes, and someone will inevitably say:

"I DON'T HAVE A CREATIVE BONE IN MY BODY."

Since it's rude to smack another adult upside the head in public, I typically *tsk, tsk* that response, point out the many ways the deluded darling is creative, and go back to eating the decorated cupcake.

Why do incredibly imaginative, bright, talented, accomplished people say—and believe—that they are not creative?

1. At some point, they were told—by someone they trusted—that they weren't creative, artistic, capable, whatever. And, for reasons both complex and simple, they took the remark to heart. A quick, snarky, "You're too tall to dance," drove one woman I know away from her beloved ballet. I could give you dozens of similar examples.

2. We all too often define (and limit) creativity as talents within the purview of artists.

LET'S DEFINE **CREATIVITY** AS **IMAGINATION IN ACTION.**

YOU HAVE AN IMAGINATION.
I HAVE AN IMAGINATION.

You take action. I take action. We create ideas, solutions, and soapbox derby cars. We make poetry and business deals and dinners. The one action we don't take often enough is giving ourselves credit for the creativity we display all the time.

That needs to change. ASAP.

Listen up and listen good: One of the 206 bones in your body is a creative bone. If you want proof, look at an X-ray. Your creative bone is right where you left it. Yep. Right there—next to your funny bone.

And I don't care if you're 6'2". Never let anyone tell you that you're too tall to dance.

Posted on Dec. 20, 2007

DANCE BETTER

Once upon a time, Gene Kelly was the choreographer for a show starring Tommy Tune. As the story goes, Kelly wasn't pleased with Tune's performance. So, he motioned the lanky dancer off to the side, and quietly said, "Dance better."

And that was all that needed to be said.

If you feel obligated to make a resolution for the year ahead, try the Kelly approach.

Write better.

/27/

Paint better.

Cook better.

Think better.

Parent better.

Drive better.

Act better.

Apologize better.

Love better.

UPDATE: Different stories vary by an inch or so, but according to the Library of Congress, Tommy Tune is 6'7". There's no dispute about this: His honors include 10 Tony Awards and the National Medal of Arts. Apparently, he is not too tall to dance.

Posted on Jan. 9, 2008

I DON'T THINK LIKE YOU THINK **I THINK**

I was in a meeting with a new client recently and he said, "You don't need to take notes on this." I laughed. I absolutely need to take notes on this, no matter what "this" is. Taking notes is how I think—it's the old reporter in me. I observe, I listen, I take notes. If I don't have a pen in my hand or a keyboard at my fingertips, my thought process is impaired.

SERIOUSLY.

Once, while presenting a media training session, I dropped my magical pen and immediately lost the ability to think. Or talk. I had no idea what to say next. Fortunately, a colleague from my agency, Jody, was presenting with me. She instantly handed me her pen, while at the same time diving under the table to pick mine up. Jody understands how I think. At that session, and throughout our friendship, her thoughtful approach has made a world of difference.

Educator, author, and creativity expert Sir Ken Robinson tells an interesting, "How do you think?" story in his "Do Schools Kill Creativity?" presentation. Robinson shares the tale of Gillian Lynne, the choreographer of *Cats* and other theatrical hits. When she was a child, teachers thought Lynne's constant fidgeting was a sign of illness.

A wise doctor determined that she wasn't sick.

She was a dancer.

Gillian Lynne thinks with movement.

/29/

WHERE AND HOW DO YOU THINK BEST?

Dancing? Driving? In the shower? Or do you generate your finest strategic and creative thoughts sitting in a chilly cubicle, unavoidably overhearing someone else's teleconference?

Determine what prompts your best thinking and embrace it. If you need a pen, grab a pen. If you need to move, move. But while you're doodling and moving, remember: Not everyone thinks the way you think. And I don't just think that. I know it.

UPDATE: In keeping with the Gillian Lynne story, there was a fascinating article in *The New York Times* years ago about an actor with cerebral palsy learning to dance. The choreographer avoided learning too much about cerebral palsy. Why? She didn't want to prejudge what he could and couldn't do.

Posted on Jan. 14, 2008

BE OPEN TO UNEXPECTED BEAUTY

Joshua Bell is one of the finest violinists in the world. He performs on a $3.5 million instrument handcrafted in 1713 by Antonio Stradivari, using a late 18th century bow by François Tourte. His music is, by any measure, astonishing. A typical ticket to one of his performances might set you back $100.

But there was that one show he did for free.

On Jan. 12, 2007, Bell gave an incognito performance in a Washington, D.C., subway station as part of a *Washington Post* story by Gene Weingarten. The reporter was interested in art and context—and Bell was willing to "play" along.

/30/

The virtuoso went to the Metro station wearing jeans and a ball cap. He pulled out that rare and wonderful violin, and started playing. You know what happened? People rushed right by him and his Stradivarius.

WHY?

Name your reason:

1. He didn't look like a virtuoso.
   He looked like a "common" street musician.

2. He had his violin case open for donations.
   People don't want to donate.

3. It was rush hour.
   People were rushing.

4. The commuters didn't hear him.
   They were on the phone, or listening to an iPod.

5. We're not children.
   Children tried to stop and listen. Parents pulled them away.

6. All of the above.

/31/

Whatever the reason, the challenge is clear:

IF WE'RE NOT RECEPTIVE TO UNEXPECTED BEAUTY

OR WISDOM OR INSIGHT OR LOVE,

WE MISS IT.

Today, make a promise to yourself:

Slow down. hook up, Listen.

There's music all around us, if only we're willing to hear it.

ADULT SWIM

Remember when you were a kid and you went to the pool and EVERY HOUR the lifeguard made you get out for the dreaded "adult swim" time?

Remember perching on the side, wondering if the lifeguard would EVER let you go back in?

Remember the pure joy of the cool water when it was FINALLY your turn to swim again?

Now, with that back-in-the-water moment in mind, choose one of these three exercises:

1. Take a photograph/draw/paint/doodle
   an image of anticipation.

2. Write one sheet, longhand,
   about your favorite summer memory.

3. Think of one activity that would
   make you feel 8 years old again. **DO IT.**

Did you make your choice? Perfect!

Now, listen carefully.

That's right: *You heard the lifeguard's whistle.*

ALL IN!

Posted on Feb. 20, 2008

CUT THE KNOT

When it comes to writing, I know what to do when I hit a knotty problem—a phrase that refuses to work, a word that doesn't fit, an idea that isn't clear. I fall back on my writer's mantra:

you own the sentence— it doesn't own you.

I stop trying to fix what isn't working. I start a new sentence.

However, I am far more comfortable with writing than I am with knitting. On the current scarf attempt, I hit the mother lode of all knots. /33/ *What was once yarn became a relentlessly twisted wreck of unforgiving fiber.*

Being a newbie knitter and a psychotic over-achiever, I refused to admit defeat. I spent hours trying to untie the knots. Hours.

Then, I finally realized: I own the yarn. It doesn't own me.

I cut the cord. Literally. Cut the knot out, tied the yarn back together, and took off knitting again. Now, this may not be the approved approach in knitting, but this is a scarf—not a nuclear power plant. One glitch won't end the world.

The next time you hit a roadblock, remember:

If at first you don't succeed, try again.

If that doesn't work? Cut the knot.

Posted on March 19, 2009

HOW TO WRITE

Think about your audience.
Read short stories.
Tell a story.
Don't wait for inspiration.
Write every day.
Rewrite.
Be specific.
Read the classics.
Edit.
Keep a journal.
Take notes.
Doodle.
/34/   Read poetry.
Listen to people.
Flip through a dictionary.
Get to the point.
Have a point.
Keep the journal with you.
Don't edit.
Go to an art gallery.
Help someone.
Keep sentences short.
Use active verbs.
Use your eraser.
Listen to music.
Go to the zoo.
Feel alive.
Go for a drive.
Know the rules.
Use the rules.
Break the rules.

But only with purpose.

A SHORT HISTORY OF YOU

In the beginning...

When my friend Maureen began the process of converting to Judaism, she took a number of classes to learn about the religion. In one of them, the instructor gave the students a concise (and oft-repeated) history of the Jewish people:

THEY TRIED TO KILL US.

WE SURVIVED.

LET'S EAT.

How would you sum up your story? Write your life history in three sentences, with no more than six words in each sentence.

If you spend more than 90 seconds getting started, you're thinking too long. *Start writing.*

Posted on June 9, 2009

WHAT ARE YOU HIDING?

Last Saturday, I spent most of the day in an XL T-shirt and a pair of shorts that are two sizes too big. Very comfy. Very me. Sunday, I bit the bullet and put on my swimsuit.

Which outfit made me look thinner? Yep, the swimsuit. I looked better when I was displaying every ounce of every curve, including the many ounces I'm still trying to lose. Go figure.

We all do this.

We all cover up something—pounds, talents, fears.

/36/   Take a chance, my friend.

Stop hiding.

Posted on Aug. 25, 2009

DON'T KICK THE CAN

I recently took Mom shopping for shoes and other necessities. The three-hour adventure sapped all her energy and all my good nature. When we got back to her apartment, this was the conversation:

MOM: The least I can do is offer you a can of pop.
There's a can in the refrigerator. Take it.

JANET: Thanks, Mom. But I don't want anything.

MOM: You could use a drink. Take it.

JANET: I'm fine, Mom. I don't want it.

/37/

MOM: It would make me feel better if you took it.

JANET: I. Don't. Want. It.

COULD I BE RUDER? NOT LIKELY.

That said, Mom believes everything happens for the best, so we'll turn this into a teaching moment: When you're on a team, everyone wants to feel like a contributor. Let them give. Take generously. And if you're tired and tempted to get hateful, can it.

By the by, I finally took the can of pop and enjoyed every refreshing sip. Mom was right. I needed it.

UPDATE: Clearly, this post does not reflect me as my best self. However, it does reflect reality. All relationships are complicated—even the ones based on love. *Hmmmm.* Especially the ones based on love.

Posted on Feb. 11, 2010

WHY DO YOU ASK?

Here's a lesson from an old reporter: The quality of the answers you receive reveals the quality of the questions you ask.

Now, depending on the topic and the person, the best question can be a simple, "Why?" *It's a wonderful question, as 3-year-olds know and adults forget.*

Often, though, the question needs to be a bit more targeted. For example, I rarely get furious. Irritated? Yes. Furious? No. It happened recently and I ranted to my friend Mark. His question back to me was perfect:

WHAT IS THE SOURCE OF YOUR ANGER?

He didn't ask me to justify my emotional reaction.
Why are you letting this upset you?

He didn't offer blanket sympathy.
Is there anything I can do to help?

Instead, he asked a question that made me stop and think—a question that elicited a long, cathartic response.

If you're not getting the feedback you'd like from people at home or at work, ask yourself this: "How could I rephrase this question?"

Posted on Sept. 27, 2011

MAKE YOUR **MARK**

A hail storm that hit our area this summer damaged the siding my husband Tom and I had installed on the house years ago. Today, a crew of three men from the siding company showed up, walked around to the back of the house, looked at the siding, and immediately said,

"THAT'S A **GONZO** WRAP."

Gonzo was the installer who put the siding on. He was an interesting dude—ponytail, skinny, solid muscles. Smoked a lot of cigarettes. He generally worked alone and he worked when he felt like it. We never knew /39/ when he'd show up. The job should have taken, maybe, a week. It took a month or more.

The thing is ... we didn't care. Because Gonzo was great. He was fun to talk with on the days he did show up and he loved his work. He took pride in every part of the job. The effort clearly paid off—years after he put the siding on, workers who had never seen the house before knew, without question, that Gonzo was the installer.

What's your Gonzo wrap? If we took the name off the writing, the photography, the baking, the strategy, the plumbing, the siding ... would anyone know it was yours?

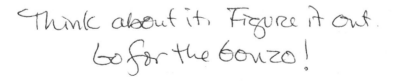

Think about it. Figure it out.
Go for the Gonzo!

Posted on July 9, 2012

LOOK AGAIN, MOM

Recently, my daughter Kate and I were driving to the mall and went past a young man, zooming along the sidewalk on his bicycle.

"He's going really fast," **I SAID.**

"He's going downhill," **KATE REPLIED.**

Now, here's the fascinating thing about that exchange: I hadn't noticed he was going downhill. Consider it part of my charm—I have the rare and wonderful ability to overlook the obvious. Fortunately for all of us, Kate adds her insight and perspective to my continually evolving thought process.

Today's advice? Surround yourself with people who see the world differently than you do. It's a *really fast* way to widen your creative vantage point. And that's a huge advantage.

Posted on Jan. 16, 2013

JUST EDIT

I just realized that I use the word just in just about every sentence I write. It's the written equivalent of a bad speech pattern.* It's also an indication that I'm stressed and feel the need to minimize whatever suggestion I am making:

- This is just an idea ...

- The attached is just a concept ...

- Just let me know if you want edits ...

Fortunately, I can rewrite:

- If this idea isn't what you had in mind, please let me know— I have others!

- I believe the attached concepts are strong ...

- Please let me know if any edits are needed.

Take a good look at what you're writing and how you're speaking. Are any bad habits sneaking in? Just edit.

* During my early days as a radio talk show host, I used to say, "OK," before every question. Every. Question. Once I realized that, I developed a new habit: Before any interview aired, I got out a razor blade and edited the tape.

Yes. You read that right. Razor blade. Tape. I'm old. But wise.

Ask me about shooting a camera with film.

Posted on April 3, 2013

STEP AWAY FROM THE SCALE

My whole life, I've measured physical success by numbers on the scale. Gain a pound or two? I'm a huge and hideous failure. Lose a pound? Yes! Time to celebrate. (Typically, with cake.)

But then something happened. I started exercising. Regularly. With Shanna (yogi, trainer, wonder worker) and the most fabulous group of women imaginable—supportive, encouraging, diverse, smart, friendly. Great people. Over the past two years:

- I lost numerous inches off various body parts.*

- I lost two dress sizes.

- I didn't lose an ounce.

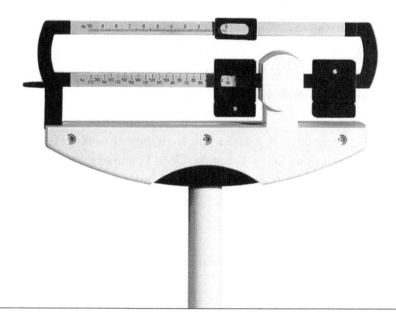

Fascinating. I look stronger, I feel healthier, and the number on the damn scale hasn't budged. Given that reality,

I DID THE MOST CREATIVE THING POSSIBLE:

I CHANGED MY MIND.

I stepped away from the scale.

HOW WE MEASURE SUCCESS MATTERS.

AND YOUR MEASUREMENT TOOL

HAS TO WORK FOR YOU.

/43/

Maybe your father wanted you to have a C-level title. Maybe your mother wanted you to marry a wealthy man. Maybe you're a CEO married to Mr. Moneybags. The folks are thrilled.

THAT'S NOT THE POINT.

Are **YOU** happy?

Do **YOU** feel successful?

Do **YOU** remember the last time you were proud of yourself?

Consider your definition of happiness and success.

If it's working for you, great!

If not, get creative. Measure better.

* No. Not those parts. For some reason, I never lose inches off those parts.

Posted on June 17, 2013

TAKE ANOTHER LOOK **AT YOURSELF**

I was out with a friend last week who is absolutely beautiful—not to mention smart, kind, all of that. We were talking about body image, and I asked her, "What's your best feature?"

She couldn't answer the question. This captivating, irresistible woman couldn't come up with anything nice to say about her appearance. Nada. Zip. Doodah. She was completely stumped.

When pushed (Who? Me? Pushy?), she finally mumbled something nice about her posture.

/44/ Then it happened again with a different friend later in the week. Once could be an oddity. Twice, and I'm sensing a trend.

Me. Fourth grade, maybe?

Cuter than I thought ☺

So, now I'm out with you. I know you are beautiful because you're reading this.

THAT MEANS YOU'RE BRILLIANT, INSIGHTFUL, AND WITTY AND—AS EVERYONE KNOWS—SMART, FUNNY PEOPLE RADIATE GOOD LOOKS.

It's true. Go look in the mirror.

After you look, come back and tell me what your best physical feature is.

I'll start.

Probably my smile. Maybe my blue eyes. My hubby might say something else ...

HAVE A GOOD TIME WHILE YOU'RE LIVING, 'CAUSE YOU'RE A LONG TIME DEAD.

END OF RETIREMENT

Right after my husband retired, our financial planner sent a document outlining how long our savings could last from first withdrawal until the *end of retirement*. I am embarrassed to tell you how long I stared at that chart, fighting disappointment over the concept that I had to go back to work in my 90s.

Fortunately, even a dim bulb shines a little light.

I did have the good grace to laugh at myself when the light went on, and I finally realized that *end of retirement* didn't mean I'd be hauling my 90-year-old tush up to the office to write ad copy again. *End of retirement* meant THE END. Done. Fini. Dead as a doornail.

I'm still laughing—the phrase may be my all-time favorite euphemism.

And yet, consider this: The dictionary defines a euphemism as a "mild or indirect word or expression substituted for one considered to be too harsh or blunt when referring to something unpleasant or embarrassing."

Has death become something that even financial planners find too "unpleasant or embarrassing" to discuss? Oy.

HERE'S MY ADVICE: When you're trying to communicate, say what you mean. Choose the right words and use the right words. Should you watch your tone? Certainly. But don't obfuscate. We have enough trouble understanding each other as it is.

End of retirement. Seriously? You're killin' me.

Posted on March 28, 2016

SQUIRREL!

I was out running errands recently and made a mistake so foolish that—well, if I told you what it was, you'd question your own sanity for reading anything I write. Suffice it to say, the only logical response to my action was, "What were you thinking?"

I'll tell you what I was thinking:

I can't believe it's already 8:15 at night and I haven't eaten yet and god I'm tired and I had no idea it would take this long to get everything done and is it really going to snow tomorrow and I'm not sure we have food for dinner and I hope Mom is feeling OK for bingo in the morning and Kate's birthday is almost here and Mary will be in this weekend and I forgot to print my work calendar for next week and I don't remember if I have a meeting on Monday so I need to check and damn why is that driver right on my tail and oh I need to buy peanut butter.

/47/

Let me take an educated guess: I'm not the only person with those brainwaves. We're all suffering from distracted living. It's SQUIRREL!* Everywhere.

I quit. I'm ready to ignore the squirrels. When I start thinking of 30 things at once, when I get distracted from the topic at hand, I'm going to stop, congratulate myself on recognizing the issue, and reel it in.

I'm also going back to the store, because I forgot the peanut butter.

* From the movie *Up.* If you haven't seen it, you need to stop reading the book this very moment and go watch the movie. Come back and finish reading later. Right after you send me a thank you note for telling you to go watch the movie.

STOP, LOOK, AND LISTEN

Today, I want you to stop, look, and listen. Consider it the adult equivalent of stop, drop, and roll. Forget whatever fires you have to put out at work or at home. Give yourself—and someone else—the gift of undivided attention.

HERE'S YOUR EXERCISE:

When someone asks, "How are you?" today, stop rushing around. Look up. Make and maintain eye contact as you answer the question. Then, return the favor. Ask how they're doing and listen to the response.

WHY DOES IT MATTER?

LISTENING REQUIRES FOCUS.
CREATIVITY THRIVES ON FOCUS.
AND, BY THE BY, SO DO WE.

Posted on June 29, 2016

EVERY **WORD** MATTERS

During a recent lunch with a group of dear friends, one of them commented that she "had *only* run one marathon."

Out of curiosity, I raced over to Google. According to the stat I found, 0.5 percent of the U.S. population has ever run a marathon. Zero. Point. Five. Percent.

In other words, my friend is a complete amazing unusual outstanding rock star.

Only she doesn't know it.

Every word matters. Far too often, words like **ONLY** and **JUST** /49/ needlessly minimize our accomplishments and weaken our sentences.

TODAY'S TIP: **RUN RIGHT PAST THOSE NASTY QUALIFIERS.**

I'M 100 PERCENT SURE YOU CAN DO IT.

FIND YOUR FOUR

While cleaning out a closet, I found a box full of old notes and clippings and a few drawings. This, this, is my self-portrait at 23 years of age.

So sad. So, so sad.

I know why, and I won't bore you with the details. I will say, men were involved.

Now, looking at this, I want to reach back and tell my dear younger self, "It gets better!"

/50/

The words that come to mind when I look at this are all negative. (Well, other than the part of my brain that says, "Damn, girl. That's not a bad self-portrait.") And that brings us to today's creativity exercise ...

My Instagram account includes a four-word bio, and all four words make me happy: Writer. Mother. Baker. Friend.

If you had only four words to describe yourself, what would they be? This is a quick exercise: Decide on your four words in the next 60 seconds. Go!

1. _____   3. _____

2. _____   4. _____

Looking for a longer creativity exercise? Draw a self-portrait. Then, put it in a box somewhere for your future self to find ... and remember.

P.S.: I'm glad I lost the despair. I wish I hadn't lost the sweater.

Posted on Sept. 21, 2016

THE SAME 24 HOURS

One of the most common anti-creativity comments is,

"I don't have time to..."

You don't have time to paint. To exercise. To read a book. To write a book. Whatever.

I saw reports this week that Archbishop Desmond Tutu, an international hero and Nobel Peace Prize winner, was in the hospital, and—while sending good thoughts his way—I remembered the glorious day 26 years ago, when he and his wife visited the University of Missouri-Kansas City (UMKC).

As a member of the university's communications team, I had the honor of escorting them for part of their stay. Archbishop Tutu glowed; his presence felt holy. His wife Leah radiated love. I have never before and never again been in the presence of anyone like them.

/51/

Why am I telling you this now? Because right after his visit, Archbishop Tutu found time to write personal notes to the UMKC staff, thanking us for our assistance.

Dear Jan,
Thank you very much for all you did to look after us during our lovely visit to your university. We enjoyed ourselves hugely.

God bless,
Desmond Cape

You want to paint, exercise, read, write, whatever? We all have 24 hours a day. It's a question of how we prioritize them.

Posted on June 7, 2017

MORNING PAGES AND MY MOJO

Before writing *Look Up*, I spent over a year working on a book proposal with an agent on the East Coast. We had a fun idea for the book; it was all about incorporating creativity into work so you'd be happy to see Monday roll around. TGIM.

When we were both satisfied with the proposal, the agent took it around to publishing houses. A few editorial boards liked the idea and my writing, but their marketing teams weren't confident I could sell 20,000 copies.

The agent reluctantly threw in the towel. I reluctantly told family and friends. And then completely lost all creative mojo.

Morning pages, described by Julia Cameron in her classic, *The Artist's Way*, helped me get back in the groove. Morning pages are a creative boost—but they're much more than that. They're a lifesaver. Simply put, they are three pages of longhand, stream-of-consciousness writing. No punctuation needed: could be grocery lists angry rants nonsensical babble dreams to do lists anything at all that pops into mind.

No matter what you do all day, do your morning pages—right when you get up. Three pages, no thinking, no editing. Pure writing.

Then, shred 'em. Absolutely, positively. Shred. Them. You're going to write things you don't want 20,000 people to read.

Trust me on this.

/53/

ARE YOU DOING YOUR 10,000 STEPS?

A reporter once asked Thomas Edison how it felt to fail 10,000 times before he found the right filament for the light bulb. Edison famously replied,

"I NEVER FAILED.
IT WAS A 10,000-STEP PROCESS."

Shine a light on your dreams.

If you took fear of failure out of the picture,
what would you be doing right now?

/54/

_____

or/and

_____

or/and

_____

or/and

_____

or/and

_____

DO IT.

:**CHAPTER THREE**:

THE MAGIC OF FRESH STARTS

SEE THE GOOD. BE THE GOOD.

Sometimes—with books, with projects, with people—you simply have to start over. And what better time for a fresh start than a new year?

The first day of the new year is magical—no doubt about it. But here's the secret we all know and forget: January 2 is magical too. And February 2. And April 7. And on and on ...

Now, granted, some days don't feel all that enchanting. The headlines may give you the impression that the world is going to heck in a handbasket (as Lillian would say). I know the feeling. That said, Mom wouldn't tolerate a shrug of the shoulders and, "It is what it is." She'd remind us that people change the world every day, and it's up to us to change it for the better.

She'd be right. And yet, knowing we have the power to take action and taking action are two very different animals.

In my living room, I keep a souvenir from Cape Cod on display, a piece of driftwood art. Carved into the wood is a query from poet Mary Oliver: "Tell me, what is it you plan to do with your one wild and precious life?"

Her life-affirming question inspires action. On this and every wild and precious day, we can choose to look up, see the beauty that surrounds us, and create more of it.

/56/

Carpe diem, dear.
then carpe the whole dang year.

LOOK! IT'S ALMOST MIDNIGHT!

My favorite New Year's Eve celebrations were the ones Mom put on for me and my brother Harry and sister Eva when we were little. (Yes, Dad was there. But the parties were Mom's doing.) There were yummy hors d'oeuvres instead of dinner; Eva was especially fond of the frozen shrimp from Safeway. Mom made mock cocktails—orange juice and Collins mix. No drink has ever tasted better. There were noisemakers and games and Dick Clark at midnight.

There was happiness for all we were and hope for all we would become—Mom and Dad were 100 percent certain their three kids would turn out special. They thought we hung the moon. Dad believed that his whole life and Mom still does.

/57/

Naturally, the reason we've done all right is because people like Mom and Dad expected nothing less. They believed in us. Now, that's a gift.

This year, **I HOPE THE PEOPLE WHO REALIZE HOW SPECIAL YOU ARE STRENGTHEN AND SUPPORT YOUR DREAMS.** May the year bring good health and good work, happiness and hope. May it be a year filled with the pleasure of companionship and the peace of solitude.

May it be a year where the joy we create honors the people we miss.

UPDATE: This was written at the end of a year that included the deaths of Peggy Harness, my sister-in-law, and Duana Linville-Dralus, my mentor. I was missing them as I wrote the post. Now, of course, Mom is gone too. And Dad. And my grandmother. And ... well, so many. I miss them all. I miss them still. The people we love stay with us, year in and year out. Just as it should be.

NO REGRETS

**IT'S BEEN SAID
THAT WE DON'T REGRET OUR MISTAKES;
WE REGRET
ALL THE THINGS WE DIDN'T DO.**

What would you like to do that you're not doing?

_____

or/and

_____

or/and

_____

What steps will you take to make it happen?

_____

or/and

_____

or/and

_____

Posted on Dec. 18, 2012

WHAT HAPPENS WHEN I LOOK UP "SILLY PUTTY"

Why was I looking up "Silly Putty" on Google? I don't know. Maybe because I keep a Silly Putty egg in my top desk drawer, and my mind was wandering. Completely possible.

No matter the reason. As Lillian would say, "Everything happens for the best." Now that I've looked it up, here's my New Year's wish for you: This year, I hope you're more like Silly Putty:

1. **WILLING TO CHANGE**—the first name was Nutty Putty.

2. **HAPPY TO HAVE THE WORD "SILLY" ASSOCIATED WITH YOUR NAME.**
   Silliness is underrated. Giggles are good.

3. **UNWILLING TO BE CONSIDERED A FAILURE.**
   Silly Putty wasn't the great replacement for synthetic rubber that GE and the government wanted. And yet ...

4. **SUCCESSFUL.**
   Millions of those Silly Putty eggs have sold, generating millions of dollars.

5. **USEFUL.**
   Grab your Silly Putty, and you're ready to prop up a chair. Pick up lint. Secure tools in zero gravity on Apollo 8. Silly Putty ain't just silly.

Most importantly, Silly Putty is resilient—and that brings us to the final part of my wish for you today: May this be a year where you bounce back fast, no matter what life hands you.

IT'S NEVER TOO LATE.

Posted on Dec. 19, 2012

MAN, THAT WAS NICE OF ME

Have you ever heard of self-cheer? It's the positive voice of self-talk, and if you haven't heard of it, you're not alone. It's not only a term most of us don't know; it's the voice we rarely hear. What we typically hear inside our overworked, overwhelmed brains is: "How could I be that stupid? Why did I do that? What was I thinking? I wasn't thinking. I'm an idiot. A complete freakin' idiot."

Oddly enough, continually telling yourself that you're a complete freakin' idiot rarely inspires great work.

So, this year, I want you to be as kind to yourself as you are to children and other people you love. I want you to say to yourself, "Brenda, you rock!" *Insert your name inside your head. You are not Brenda. Unless you are Brenda. In which case, you know who you are and you do rock.*

/61/

OTHER SELF-CHEERS?

"I'm brilliant."
"What I just accomplished? Amazing."
"I may be the best (father, lover, writer, whatever) in the universe."
"Man, that was nice of me."

We can make it super simple: The next time you do something great, say to yourself, "Good job!" Heck, you could do that a million times during the day: You get up on time. "Good job!" You have clean clothes to wear. "Good job!" You arrive at the meeting with all your notes. "Good job!" You don't make the snarky comment you'd like to make to the boss, significant other, or 10,001 social media connections. "Good job!"

THIS WEEK, THIS MONTH, THIS YEAR,

DO A GOOD JOB.

BE A COMPLETE FREAKIN' CHEERLEADER. FOR YOURSELF.

START A **SMILE FILE**

At times, you'll doubt yourself. We all do. When doubt strikes, it's good to remember how wonderful others think you are. How? Create a "smile file." I use this fun envelope for my smile file, but any folder works. You only have a plain manila envelope? Terrific. Doodle on the outside—it's the perfect medium for a smile file design.

What goes in the file? Emails with compliments. Great job reviews. Valentines. That kind of thing. Whatever you get that brings a smile and/or makes you feel talented and appreciated. If you're not sure what to put in your smile file first, no worries.

Scan the next page, print it, file it - and you've begun!

Way to go! You're
Getting in touch w/
your best creative self.
I think you rock.

Hugs—Jan

Jan Harness

Chief Creative Instigator

/64/

YOU DESERVE BETTER.

Posted on Dec. 31, 2016

MY WISH FOR YOU

Be Kind.

Be kind to yourself.

To those around you.

To strangers.

Be kind to people who look like you, and those who don't.

To people who share your beliefs, and those who don't.

Be kind to the helpers:
the clerk, the plumber, the policeman, the waiter.

To teachers.

To your neighbors, your family.

Be kind to animals.

And, because it bears saying one more time: Be kind to yourself.

Kindness is magic.

One kind word can transform a day.

One kind person can transform a life.

One kind community can transform the world.

/65/

UPDATE: On this page and throughout the book, I frequently say, "Be kind." Repeating a key message is, well, key. People are busy. Multi-tasking. Multi-stressed. Periodically repeating* the message you most want to communicate significantly increases the chance that your audience will grasp what you're saying. Consider that the next time you talk to your kid. Or your significant other.

* Spoiler alert: I've been known to cross the fine line between repeating and browbeating.

**WHEN WE TALK ABOUT FRESH STARTS,
I'M DOUBLY LUCKY.**

I celebrate the secular New Year and the Jewish New Year, known as Rosh Hashanah. Of course, Jewish guilt being what it is, we follow that celebration with Yom Kippur, the Day of Atonement. On Yom Kippur, Jews around the world recite the Ashamnu, an alphabetized confessional prayer. This poem is my updated version of that prayer.

ASHAMNU: MY ALPHABET OF FAILINGS

For the sin of **ANGER** against those who challenge me
And for the sin of **BELITTLING** those I don't understand

For the sin of **CRITICIZING** without caring
And for the sin of **DOUBTING** the strength of love

For the sin of **ENJOYING** what I shouldn't have
And for the sin of purposefully **FINDING** fault

For the sin of **GREED** when I have so much
And for the sin of **HARBORING** resentment

For the sin of needlessly **IMAGINING** problems
And for the sin of **JOKING** to avoid a truth.

*For all these sins, O God of forgiveness,
Forgive me, pardon me, grant me atonement.*

For the sin of **KINDNESS** too often withheld
And for the sin of **LOVING** in measured touches

For the sin of **MALICE** toward those who are richer
And for the sin of **NOURISHING** my worst intentions

For the sin of **OBSERVING** when I could be helping
And for the sin of **PRETENDING** I am less than I am

For the sin of **QUITTING** when I still have fight
And for the sin of not **RESTING** when I am exhausted

For the sin of **SAYING** it doesn't matter
And for the sin of **THINKING** they can read my mind.

For all these sins, O God of forgiveness,
Forgive me, pardon me, grant me atonement.

For the sin of not cutting the **UMBILICAL** cord
And for the sin of not **VISITING** my parents enough

For the sin of not **WEEPING**, to prove my strength
And for the sin of never forgiving my **EX**

For the sin of **YEARNING** to alter time
And for the sin of repenting at the **ZERO** hour.

For all these sins, O God of forgiveness,
Forgive me, pardon me, grant me atonement.

Ashamnu was published online in 2016 by the Union for Reform Judaism, and was incorporated into Yom Kippur services at various congregations around the country. In 2017, the *Kansas City Jewish Chronicle* published the poem as part of its High Holy Days special edition. And, in a move that would have thrilled my very religious father beyond belief, Stephen Wise Temple in Los Angeles—one of the largest synagogues in the world—included it in the *Stephen Wise Temple High Holy Days Machzor*, published in 2019. (*Machzor* is the Hebrew word for the High Holy Days prayer book.)

IT MIGHT HAVE BEEN

Ready to fire off a few new synapses, courtesy of a few old memories? Rather than doodling this in the book, you need to take out a clean sheet of paper. You'll see why. Ready? Go!

1. Write down three things you've lost:

   One object

   One person

   One belief

2. Write one sentence about each

3. Choose the lost item that feels most important right now

4. Write why that loss matters, and why or if you would like to have the object/person/belief back

5. Consider these lines from John Greenleaf Whittier:

   For all sad words of tongue or pen,
   The saddest are these: "It might have been!"

6. Rip the paper into tiny shreds. If you want. Or frame it. You'll know what to do.

Every day gives us a fresh start, a chance to look up from day-to-day life, and gain a new perspective on our future.

Who knows what it might be?

THERE ARE OTHER FISH IN THE SEA.

Posted on Dec. 29, 2017

LOSE THE RIGHT WEIGHT

Since I am the only Jewish momma many of you have, I feel obligated to tell you the truth. In the new year, you do need to lose that weight.

You need to lose the weight of the world. Your shoulders are strong and beautiful. They were never meant to carry the universe. Keep doing what you can to make our world a better place; we need you more than ever. But, as you do, remember that the world will keep spinning even if you stop pushing.

You need to lose the weight of the past. You made mistakes. You didn't do your best. You spoke in anger. Maybe you messed up this year. Maybe you're still fretting about something from decades ago. Or, perhaps the weight you bear stems from another's action. Someone wounded you, abused you, broke you. No matter what your past burden, dear heart, let this be the year you let it go.

You need to lose the weight of expectations. I don't know if it's your expectations weighing you down or expectations imposed upon you. I do know that fear of failure can paralyze progress. This year, expect to do your best. Do it. And applaud your effort regardless of the results. Step by step gets you where you're going.

As we look ahead, let's stop measuring success by how many pounds we lose. Let's measure success by how many lives we enrich. Let's measure success by how generously we give, how wholeheartedly we laugh, how deeply we love.

THIS YEAR AND EVERY YEAR,
LET'S BE KIND TO EACH OTHER.
LET'S BE KIND TO OURSELVES.

Here's to a happy, healthy year for all of us. May you lose what you need to lose, find what you hope to find, and pause long enough to remember: It really is a wonderful world.

/71/

KISS A BUBBLE

My sister Eva will happily tell you that I am the creative one in the family. My sister Eva is wrong.

Here's an idea she "borrowed" from someone and gave to me: When you're blowing bubbles with kids, encourage them to kiss the bubbles. Get ready for laughs. Kissing the bubbles adds a giggle-gathering layer of active fun to the game.

WHAT? YOU NEVER BLOW BUBBLES? WHEN DID YOU STOP? AND WHY?

Fortunately, even if you don't have bubbles, you can still have fun.

Take something you do all the time, and change the sensory experience.

Add music, a touch, a taste, a smell.

A kiss.

You figure it out.

I'm all set.

I have bubbles.

CHAPTER FOUR

CREATIVITY ≠ CHAOS

LOOK AROUND YOU

Lillian Sokoloff was many things. *Tidy* wasn't on top of the list—and I am my mother's daughter.

If I look up from the computer and survey my desk, well ... there's everything you would expect: papers, datebook, pens, paperclips. Now, pile on top of that the assorted accoutrements of my life: shells and rocks from favorite beaches, my secret snack stash, Happy Meal toys, Groucho glasses. A perpetual calendar, perpetually on the wrong date. Bubbles.

IT AIN'T PRETTY.

Fortunately, after years and years of writing at this desk, I know my limits. Before the flat space completely disappears, I'll have to stop and clean so my brain can fully function.

How about you? What sparks your best work?

Google "creativity and chaos" and you'll find data supporting both sides of the argument—messy environments spark creative thought vs. mess creates stress. This is my book, so you get my take, based on years of completely non-scientific research. The multi-tasking, app-assaulting universe we live in is chaotic enough. Order, in our environment and work, provides:

/74/

1. **STRUCTURE** to get us going
2. **SIMPLICITY** to keep us on track
3. **SUPPORT** to know when to stop

Ahhh.

Alliteration incites tidy writing.

And I do love a list.

Posted on May 25, 2010

YOU KNOW YOU'RE A WRITER IF ...

1. You hear an NPR reporter say, "brickmaking in Pakistan," and you think: "Wow! That would be a great title for a book. *Brickmaking in Pakistan.*"

2. You notice grammatical errors on billboards.

3. You want to fix grammatical errors on billboards with red spray paint.

4. You hear the woman in front of you at Starbucks say, "no love lost," and you think: "Wow! That would be a great title for a poem. *No Love Lost.*" *(*Score! *See the next page.)*

5. **YOU THINK IN COPY.**
   If I need to explain this, subtract two points from your final score.

   /75/

6. You think of Thomas Wolfe when someone says, "You can't go home again."

7. You understand literary references even when the people who make them don't.

8. You hear a child at a funeral say, "I have tears in my heart, but I just can't get them to my eyes," and you write that down immediately, because it's perfect.

9. You **C A N** write it down immediately, because you always carry a notebook and pen.

10. The notebook you always carry is a Moleskine.
    A black Moleskine.
    Yes? You get two extra points for your extreme sophistication, style, and class. And you get three extra points if you noticed that I messed up the parallel structure of my list by not starting this with **Y O U.**

AFTER SIGNING THE PAPERS

I heard someone say
"No love
lost between them.

No love lost."
And, passing by, you

hesitated.

Then walked away.
You and I

know love
lost.

Love lost.

Posted on Dec. 2, 2010

EIGHT CREATIVITY BOOSTS

As I write this, it's the first day of Chanukah. Which means last night was the first night, since Jewish holidays begin at sunset. If you think that's confusing, try to remember the right way to put the candles in the Chanukah menorah, and the right way to light them. There are rules for everything.

Are there rules for creativity? Sure! In honor of the eight days of Chanukah, here are eight boosts that always help me:

1. **GET MOVING.** Creativity requires action. Having an imaginative idea is one step in the right direction—and not always the first step. Creativity, creating, requires implementation.

2. **BREATHE.** *This is your brain. This is your brain on oxygen.* Are you rested? Are you exercising? Are you taking care of you? Breathe in, breathe out. /77/

3. **BELIEVE IN YOUR OWN TALENTS.** Surround yourself with people who believe in you, too.

4. **PRACTICE EVERY DAY.** Creativity is craft. The more you write, love, paint, parent, bake, coach ... the better.

5. **EXPERIMENT.** There are approximately 80 gazillion ways to be creative. If writing **DOESN'T** bring you joy, try something else. If writing **DOES** bring you joy, try something else. You never know where you'll find talents and happiness.

6. **CONNECT THE DOTS.** Let the skills you've learned shooting photos help you edit copy. Approach a medical appointment as though it were a meeting with your child's teacher. Ask yourself, "How would I do this if ..."

7. **STEP AWAY FROM THE COMPUTER.** Give your brain a break. Look up. Then, step away from everything and everyone. Just be.

8. **GO FOR THE GOAL.** We move toward what we see. See the happy ending.

During a class I took years ago at a summer session of the Iowa Writers'
Workshop, the instructor would periodically give us random rules.

For example, write a poem that includes at least five colors.
That atypical (for me) structure led to this poem.

WIDOW

I used to be someone else
Before the white flash of certainty
Stopped me on a summer morning.

Sunlight steamed through our bathroom window.
The hairdryer unplugged itself, falling from my hands.
I grabbed the phone and dialed by heart,
Overland Park Medical Center, 3rd floor east, nurses' station.

7:32 a.m. Sue was on duty.
Sue, with the pretty blond hair and the gentle blue eyes,
The one you preferred for drawing blood.

"We're giving him CPR," she said. "They're in with him right now."

I wish I could say I rushed to the hospital.
Or woke the children. Or called your mother.
Instead, I stood perfectly still, willing the moment to disappear.

Wrapping myself tighter in the pink and grey towel you never liked,
I stared at your pillow on our double bed,
Saw you folding your pajamas and tucking them under,
One final, comforting routine before another overnight treatment.

They left you in the room until I got there,
The fan turned on high to keep us both cool.
Your pale head, carefully positioned on their pillows.

The silky grey voices of doctors drifted through,
Condolences and explanations.

I listened. Or I didn't.
I answered. Or I didn't.
I laughed when there was no reason.

I never cried
Until leaving the wet brown dirt of your grave,
Joey introduced me to a distant cousin,
Not as your wife,
But your widow.

THINK PINK

The next time you head out for a walk or run, look for the color blue.

> Or yellow.

> Or orange.

> Or pink!

Search for items in that color. Look for your color on the neighbor's house, the car at the curb, the dented street sign at the corner. You'll be amazed where it pops up.

> Why are you suddenly seeing red? (Or pink or blue or green?)

FOCUS.

> Focusing our attention empowers us to see things that otherwise blend into the day-to-day background.

> The rainbow is always there; it's our perspective that changes.

IN LIFE AND ON WALKS, WE SEE WHAT WE SEEK.

Posted on Jan. 6, 2013

EMBRACE STRUCTURE

Back when I was in school, professors would periodically assign long papers, complete with outlines. My classmates and I had to turn in our outlines first. Unfortunately, my brain doesn't think in outlines.

I handled it the only way I could: backwards. I'd write the entire paper, then go back and create the outline. On the bright side, I always finished those papers early. No outline required? Yes! I wrote those papers the night before they were due. My brain does think in deadlines.

Over the years, I've learned to embrace the concept of structure. The trick is finding a structure that resonates. For example, when I wrote *Creative Chai*, an e-book to accompany my creativity presentations, the chapter structure of 18* ideas kept me focused. Numbers, whether deadlines or headlines, work for me.

What structure works for you? When you set a goal or make a resolution, do you build that structure into the plan?

If you're not sure where to start, consider a pre-existing structure. For example, my daughter Kate is taking and posting a daily photo as part of a Project 365 adventure.

Let structure be the bones of your creative endeavor. Now, build!

* Chai stands for both *18* and *life* in Hebrew.

Posted on Nov. 19, 2013

THANK YOU, THANK YOU, THANK YOU!

Here's a tip before you read this primer on thank you notes: There is a test at the end. So, sit up straight and pay attention. You'll thank me later.

1. **HAVE STATIONERY* ON HAND** so you're ready to put pen to paper. That's right. Pen to paper. You might think it's a lost art, but it's making a comeback—and you can be part of the trend. If you're thinking, "I'll just send a quick email or text," that's fine for acknowledging receipt of a gift. But nothing replaces a note in the mail.

2. **BE PROMPT.** Write the note within a day or two of receiving the gift, enjoying the dinner out, whatever. "Within a day or two" is not Emily Post etiquette—I'm sure you have longer than that to still be correct. However, the longer you put it off, the less likely you are to write it. And, unfortunately, the longer you put it off, the more likely you are to approach composing the note like a task, rather than a genuine expression of gratitude.

3. **MAKE IT A GENUINE EXPRESSION OF GRATITUDE.** Stop for a minute and think about why this is nice, what the gift/event means to you, what the person means to you, etc.

4. **DON'T WORRY ABOUT THE SALUTATION.** Dear "Name" is always appropriate. Or, have fun if you want— for example, *Pattibeth!* As opposed to *Dear Patricia.* (Again, I am not Emily Post.)

5. **DON'T WORRY ABOUT WORD COUNT.** It's fine to keep the note short and sincere. (I'm 5 feet tall. I avoid the phrase, "Short and sweet.") Short is probably best. It's a thank you, not a term paper. On the other hand, this is no time for a tweet. *Thanks a lot!* is not enough.

6. **BE SPECIFIC.** Mention the item or event, and a reason or two why it is special. For example:

Dear Ken,

Thank you for the wonderful lunch at (yakka bakka restaurant name here). The company was spectacular and the food was delicious. It was incredibly thoughtful of you to tell the hostess ahead of time that it was my birthday—dessert is always a treat. As is time with you!

With love and gratitude,

Jan

/83/

7. **WRAP IT UP.** Consider any of these perfectly fine sign-offs: *Thanks again, Cheers, All the best, With gratitude, In appreciation, Love, Sincerely,* or the basic and always appropriate *Thank you!*

NOW, THE TEST

Hey, I warned you. Look around and find a present someone gave you a long, long time ago. Something that you have kept, treasured, etc. For example, I keep a framed photo on my desk that *mybestfriendinthewholeworldsincefourthgrade* Lynn sent me years ago—a photo of us on vacation, in a frame that has special meaning.

Did you find something? Great. Now, write a thank you note to the person who gave it to you. And don't forget to mail it.

* Also, keep a dictionary on hand so you can look up *stationery* vs. *stationary.*

DROP AND GIVE ME 17. SYLLABLES.

To instigate a little creativity today, I want you to write a haiku. It's easy: If you can count, you can write haiku. If you can't count, well. Yes. Moving on ...

Follow the haiku formula. The first line has five syllables, the second line has seven syllables, the third line has five syllables. Here are two examples I wrote, and *Longing*, a brilliant bonus from designer Jo Bittel.

STATIC

Driving in my car,
radio cranked, windows down,
your voice still comes through.

Longing

Long, long time ago
happiness resonated
time to be happy.

SONG OF MY CITY

blue fried whiskey jazz
born to smoke slow and tender
Kansas City sings.

There are 17 zillion 17-syllable possibilities. Write one.

Static was published in *The Kansas City Star*.

Song of My City was published in *Star* magazine.

15 FABULOUS FAVORITES: BOOKS

August 2017 marks 15 years since I decided to ignore conventional wisdom *(Don't quit your day job!)* and launch Sokoloff Harness Communications LLC. I am tremendously grateful to everyone who has helped me along the way and to those who have given me the honor of helping them. My big advice after 15 years?

DON'T QUIT YOUR DAY DREAM.

In honor of the 15th anniversary, I'm delighted to present a couple lists of 15 fabulous favorites—starting, of course, with books. Now, keep in mind, a list of favorite books is a moving target. This is today's list. Read fast. It could change tomorrow.

1. **LITTLE WOMEN** by Louisa May Alcott
   Life changing. I still want to be Jo.

2. **CAN'T WE TALK ABOUT SOMETHING MORE PLEASANT?** by Roz Chast
   Drawn from her life. And mine. And quite possibly yours.

3. **THIS IS HOW YOU LOSE HER** by Junot Díaz
   I have several of his other books and don't like them as well. But this one would make my five favorite books of all-time list.

4. **THE SCARLET LETTER** by Nathaniel Hawthorne
   I could have listed *Siddhartha* or *The Odyssey* or *Les Miserables* ... or any of the books I still have that I read in my lit classes at Center Senior High School. Thank you, Miss Harvey and Mrs. Harper. I'm sorry I argued with you. I'm sure you were right about that symbolism.

5. **HYPERBOLE AND A HALF** by Allie Brosh
I love the book. You can start with the blog.
Best description of depression EVER.

6. **THE SIRENS OF TITAN** by Kurt Vonnegut
Vonnegut is the best-represented author on my bookshelves.
I chose this Vonnegut book because, as I remember,
it was the first one I read.

7. **THE EDEN EXPRESS** by Mark Vonnegut
A remarkable memoir by the elder Vonnegut's son.
Excellent writing runs in the family.

8. **THE DIARY OF A YOUNG GIRL** by Anne Frank
Also life changing—nothing like reading this as a
young Jewish girl, Anne's age.

9. **i carry your heart with me** by E. E. Cummings
My favorite poem, in book form, illustrated by mati mcdonough.

10. **THE YEAR OF MAGICAL THINKING** by Joan Didion
If you've ever lost a loved one and you haven't read this book—
read it.

11. **THE POCKET BOOK OF MODERN VERSE**
edited by Oscar Williams
My first true love gave me this and it includes a few of
my all-time favorite poems, including *Cascando* by
Samuel Beckett and *A Space in the Air* by Jon Silkin.
Since Robert Frost is in there, I won't list a Frost collection.

12. **SAMURAI WIDOW** by Judith Jacklin Belushi
Fascinating journey through grief and recovery.

13. **WAITING FOR GODOT** by Samuel Beckett
Reading and discussing this in college was the first
time I went: "Oh. That professor makes sense.
This play isn't boring. It's brilliant."
Thank you, Mrs. Ehrlich.
You transformed my literary vision.

14. **THE ASSOCIATED PRESS STYLEBOOK**
Am I a word nerd? Yes. Do I like rules? Yes.

/87/

Do I look at this book all the time? Yes.

Why clutter up my mind with **EFFECT** and **AFFECT**
when I have my trusty stylebook?

15. **THE BOBBSEY TWINS** by Laura Lee Hope
My Bobbsey Twin will understand—as she has,
from the days when my love for books began.

UPDATE: This book was edited using a "house style" blend of
The Associated Press Stylebook and *Dreyer's English, An Utterly
Correct Guide to Clarity and Style* by Benjamin Dreyer. All mistakes
and inconsistencies are mine. I've been writing and editing long
enough to know there will be mistakes, no matter how many times
I proofread the book—or how many eagle-eyed editors review it.

Fortunately, I've also taken enough yoga classes to realize that
perfection is not the most realistic of goals.

DON'T READ IN THE DARK.

BRANCH OUT

It's time for something new.

Go to your local library, one of the finest inventions ever. If you don't have a library card, smack yourself upside the head, then get one. If you do have a library card, bypass the thump and proceed to the stupendous stacks of beautiful books.

Now, choose a genre you never or rarely read. Biography, science fiction, history, Western, whatever. If being out of your literary element makes you twitchy, switch from novels to short stories.

READ.

You never know how or when a word, line, paragraph, or story will inspire you. And remember the Stephen King quote, "If you don't have the time to read, you don't have the time or tools to write."

Posted on Aug. 15, 2017

FIVE WAYS TO SMASH WRITER'S BLOCK

Never, never, never, never, never.

Well, almost never.

That's how often I have writer's block when it comes to client copy. I'm a professional writer; I can't wait for inspiration to hit—deadlines hit on a daily basis. This is a good thing. But ...

This week, I've been struggling to finish a book proposal. We're down to the final version. My agent wants two more sample chapters and a few minor edits. No problem, right?

Well, the first additional chapter was easy to write. The edits were easy to make. And then, AIEEEEEEEEEEEEEE! Writer's block gone crazy. A chapter that should have taken two hours to write took two days. And I'm still not ready to say it's done.

Since Lillian says everything happens for the best, I went looking for a silver lining. And I found one: The experience did give me five great tips for smashing writer's block:

1. Rather than giving up, **GET UP.** Leave the computer, the tablet, the notebook, whatever you're writing on and walk away. Inspiration is like love; it shows up when you're not looking for it.

2. Do something that forces you to think of other things. I like to **GO FOR A DRIVE.** I have to focus on my driving, because I have absolutely no innate sense of direction.*

3. If you, like me, have words on the page but you're sure they stink, look again. Is the lead hidden in paragraph four? First paragraphs are often triggers—necessary to get going, but then you need to pull them. Do it. **CUT YOUR COPY.**

4. **GET PHYSICAL.** Your brain may not be working the way you'd like, but there's that beautiful body of yours! Use it. Exercise. Do something you enjoy. Or, go to sleep—that may be just what your body needs.

5. Stop beating yourself up. We can't be brilliant 24/7. **HAVE FAITH.** The words you're searching for will find you.

/91/

KEEP SHINING
BEAUTIFUL ONE
THE WORLD NEEDS
YOUR LIGHT.

* Truly.

No sense of direction whatsoever.

Ask my *mybestfriendinthewholeworldsincefourthgrade* about this. Better yet, don't ask. Why make her relive our navigational nightmares?

Posted on Aug. 16, 2017

18 WAYS TO BE A MENSCH

Wonder what a "mensch" is and why you'd want to be one? Essentially, "mensch" is a fabulous Yiddish word for a solid, thoughtful, kind human being. To explain it in reverse: At a restaurant, a person who is nice to the people she's dining with, but rude to the waiter is *not* a mensch. Don't be that person.

1. **BE NICE** to the waiter.

2. Follow the advice from Sai Baba, an Indian spiritual master:
   **"BEFORE YOU SPEAK, ASK YOURSELF:
   IS IT KIND, IS IT NECESSARY, IS IT TRUE?
   DOES IT IMPROVE UPON THE SILENCE?"**
   (I've also seen this quote attributed to Buddha.
   And, oddly enough, Yogi Bear.)

3. Hold doors open, especially for the elderly or people with arms full of packages or babies. Smile as you let them go through.

4. When you make a mistake, **APOLOGIZE. GRACIOUSLY.**
   Face-to-face, if possible, and with no excuses.
   The "no excuses" part is critical.

5. **PUT YOUR PHONE AWAY.** Look up. Pay attention to the person right in front of you.

6. Look for the lonely people. Let them know you're there, if they want to talk.

7. Say, "Thank you!" **SAY, "YOU'RE WELCOME!** My pleasure."
   (There's a huge difference between this response and the unfortunately ubiquitous, "No problem.")

8. **LET SOMEONE ELSE WIN.** Let them have the worst day.
   Or the best recipe.

9. Don't go for the easy joke if it might hurt someone's feelings.

10. Think about the other person's feelings.

11. **REMEMBER THAT EVERYONE—EVERYONE— IS STRUGGLING WITH SOMETHING.** Since this is a post on being a *mensch*, I'll continue with the Yiddish. We all have *tsurris* (troubles, disasters, heartache). We all have *mishegas* (craziness).

12. Offer help to someone who is struggling, without waiting to be asked.

13. Go beyond letting the other driver cut in front of you during rush hour. Be a real mensch. Don't flip him off.

14. Visit someone who is ill.

15. Surprise a neighbor with homemade goodies.

16. **SHOW UP.** Attend the weddings. Attend the funerals.

17. Listen to the answer—or the silence—when you ask someone how they're doing.

18. Put decency, human dignity, and respect first. Always. And remember, that underpaid waiter is every bit as deserving of decency, dignity, and respect as you are.

Posted on Aug. 18, 2017

15 FABULOUS FAVORITES: QUOTES

In 2002, my sweet sister Eva took me to a women's health conference in Columbia, Mo. The heart of the keynote speaker's presentation came down to one essential question: "What would you do today if you were brave?"

WORDS MATTER. WORDS CHANGE LIVES. THAT QUESTION CHANGED MINE.

As I drove back to Kansas City, I knew what I would do. And, with support from family and friends, I did it. I opened the doors to my own communications agency.

/94/ Given the power of words, it's only fitting to do a Fabulous 15 list of favorite quotes. I hope you find one here that speaks to your heart.

1. **WHEREVER YOU GO, GO WITH ALL YOUR HEART.**
Confucius. I love this line; it's on my business cards.

2. **THOUGH SHE BE BUT LITTLE, SHE IS FIERCE.**
Shakespeare. Self-explanatory, if you've met me.
If not, I'm really close to 5 feet tall. Really close. Really.
Don't question this, or the rest of the quote will also become self-explanatory.

3. **WE WRITE. WE TALK. THAT'S WHAT JEWISH WOMEN DO. WE KISS WORDS.**
We kiss words. Three is magic.
By Susan Schnur in the magazine *Lilith*.

4. **PEOPLE CHANGE, AND FORGET TO TELL EACH OTHER.**
Lillian Hellman. And she was right.

5. **THE ONLY THING NECESSARY FOR THE TRIUMPH OF EVIL IS FOR GOOD MEN TO DO NOTHING.**

   Edmund Burke. Completely true. So do something.

6. **IF YOU REST, YOU RUST.**

   Helen Hayes. She's gone, but she didn't rust away.

7. **EVERYTHING HAPPENS FOR THE BEST.**

   Lillian Sokoloff. Vastly different than the popular *Everything happens for a reason*. When I was a kid, the family went to Galveston and Dad locked the keys in the car. The locksmith who came to help saw our Star of David medallion on the dashboard—turned out, he was anti-Semitic. He and Dad almost got into a fistfight. When he finally left, the three of us kids turned to Mom and demanded to know what happened for the best. And she said, "We got to stay a little longer at the beach."

   /95/

8. **TO LAUGH OFTEN AND MUCH; TO WIN THE RESPECT OF INTELLIGENT PEOPLE AND THE AFFECTION OF CHILDREN; TO EARN THE APPRECIATION OF HONEST CRITICS AND ENDURE THE BETRAYAL OF FALSE FRIENDS; TO APPRECIATE BEAUTY; TO FIND THE BEST IN OTHERS; TO LEAVE THE WORLD A BIT BETTER WHETHER BY A HEALTHY CHILD, A GARDEN PATCH, OR A REDEEMED SOCIAL CONDITION; TO KNOW EVEN ONE LIFE HAS BREATHED EASIER BECAUSE YOU HAVE LIVED. THIS IS TO HAVE SUCCEEDED.**

   Ralph Waldo Emerson. I've adopted his definition of success as mine. (Different sources differ on a word or two of this quote, but the essence remains.)

9. **THE FUTURE BELONGS TO THOSE WHO BELIEVE IN THE BEAUTY OF THEIR DREAMS.**
Eleanor Roosevelt. I wonder what she would have
been like as president.

10. **MEASURE TWICE. CUT ONCE.**
Yiddish wisdom. I come from a family of tailors.

11. **IN THREE WORDS, I CAN SUM UP EVERYTHING I'VE LEARNED ABOUT LIFE: IT GOES ON.**
Robert Frost. It does. Life goes on.
Even when you feel like it shouldn't.

12. **AT THE MOMENT OF COMMITMENT, THE UNIVERSE CONSPIRES TO ASSIST YOU.**
By Goethe, maybe? Not sure. But I am sure that it's true.
And it's a lovely conspiracy.

13. **NO ACT OF KINDNESS, NO MATTER HOW SMALL, IS EVER WASTED.**
Aesop. Truth.

14. **NOT ALL WHO WANDER ARE LOST.**
I love the J.R.R. Tolkien line and the poem it comes from,
including this stanza:

"All that is gold does not glitter,
  Not all those who wander are lost;
  The old that is strong does not wither,
  Deep roots are not reached by the frost."

15. **I STILL BELIEVE THAT PEOPLE ARE GOOD AT HEART.**
Anne Frank. And if she could believe it, we should believe it.

CHAPTER FIVE:

THE POWER OF PRESENCE
HERE I AM

As I mention in the intro to *Look Up*, my first title for this book was *Hineni*, a Hebrew word meaning *Here I am.*

It doesn't mean: "Here I am, standing in front of you, staring at my phone."

HINENI MEANS,
"HERE I AM. I SEE YOU. I HEAR YOU.
I AM FULLY PRESENT."

How glorious is that? When was the last time you looked up—from the phone, the computer, the iPad, the book—and gave someone your full attention? When was the last time someone else reciprocated?

I was reminded of the importance of presence, of focus, when watching the last episode of the first season of *The Kominsky Method* on Netflix—the scene where the characters demonstrate the acting exercise of mirroring. You may have done it as a kid: Two people pair off, one partner moves, the other partner precisely mirrors the action. Doing this successfully requires complete concentration on the other person. As Sandy Kominsky, the Michael Douglas character, notes, the effort involved in being fully present makes you a better actor. And a better person.

We can apply that same lesson to writing, painting, making dinner. You can't be fully creative if you're not fully present. You can't be your best self if you're not fully present.

As family and friends periodically point out, I am *extremely* distracted by shiny objects. However, I do have one advantage when it comes to tapping the power of presence: I'm half deaf. If I don't pay attention, I miss things.

Knowing that, I focus on the people and activities around me. I learned to lip read as a child (the doctors were afraid I might go profoundly deaf), and developed a habit then of observing people's faces.

Turns out, it's a lovely habit. I've gained the opportunity to truly see—and hear—intriguing people throughout my life. We all want to be seen, you know. We want to be heard.

And we all have _stories_ to tell.

Hineni, my friend. Here I am, happy to share a few stories that have shaped my life, my work, and my creativity—and hoping the lessons I've learned along the way help you.

NO ANSWER IS ALSO AN ANSWER.

THE **DELIGHT** IS IN THE **DETAILS**

Happy day! Let's get your mind in motion.

- Think of a favorite place.

- Write 10 details about that place.

- Incorporate three of those details into a poem! Or a painting.

For example, I'm thinking of my grandmother's kitchen:

1. The kitchen was in the back of the house.

2. The house was at 5721 Holmes.

3. The kitchen was long and narrow, with lots of cupboards.

4. If you entered from the formal dining room, the sink was on the right and the stove was on the left. There was an eat-in area at the back, by the steps to the basement.

5. Windows over the sink overlooked the adjoining driveways between my grandmother's house and the neighbor's house.

6. My grandmother wrote "Milk" and "Meat" inside the cupboards and drawers so no one would mess up her kosher kitchen.

7. There was a poem, cut out from the newspaper's Dear Abby or Ann Landers column, posted in the kitchen. I can't remember the entire poem, but the gist was, "Please stay out of my kitchen. And when I am invited to your house, I promise to stay out of yours." Nanny didn't like interlopers in the kitchen. She didn't want help. This was her space.

/101/

8. She didn't mind me in the kitchen, because I sat on the handmade stool in the corner, watching her cook and quietly listening as she talked.

9. Toward the end of her life, when she didn't have enough strength to stand at the sink and do food prep or wash dishes, Nanny pulled up a tall stool and did the work sitting down.

10. Nanny twinkled.

Now, here's the wonderful thing about this exercise. I knew, before I started the list, that I would talk about the structure of the kitchen and the poem and my stool in the corner. I had no idea about #10. Because, until I got there, I had sort of forgotten how Nanny twinkled.

And that's not something I want to forget.

THE FIRST PASSOVER WITHOUT YOU

I drop matzah balls in boiling broth,
watch them float,
bobbing like family against each other
touching, moving, together,

apart.

Tonight, we'll light the candles,
read the haggadah,
open the door to our home for Elijah,
the only ghost at the Seder

until now.

Posted on Feb. 14, 2008

THAT'S SOME VALENTINE

A kid is lucky to have one great mother. I was doubly blessed. Not only do I have the world's best mom, but when Lynn Dougherty and I became best friends for life in fourth grade, Lynn's mom took me under her wing.

Her presence was a gift. Joyce Dougherty was one of the most creative women I ever knew. Whether she was painting, stitching, or cooking, she was an artist.

She was also a cigarette-smoking, no-fools-tolerating spitfire, with rock-solid Southern manners. If that sounds like a contradiction, I'm guessing you've never been to North Carolina.

/103/

I want to share one of Mrs. Dougherty's favorite lines—one that you can use in any number of awkward situations:

THAT'S SOME BABY!

What do you say when a proud new mama shows you the world's ugliest newborn? "That's some baby!" What do you say when a friend decorates a less-than-Martha-Stewart cake? "That's some cake!" And what do you say when your lover gives you a completely inappropriate Valentine?

You got it.

Happy Valentine's Day!
From me. And Mrs. Dougherty.

Posted on June 24, 2008

GIVING CREDIT WHERE CREDIT IS DU

In 1986, I left an eight-year stint in radio news at KUDL-FM and WHB-AM and started work at the University of Missouri-Kansas City. The academic environment was a culture shock: It was definitely not the wacky world of radio. Fairly quickly, I was convinced I had made a huge mistake.

As I poked around my basement office, dejectedly considering how I could get my old job back, I heard this humongous laugh echoing through Scofield Hall. I followed the sound upstairs, walked into the laughing woman's office, and asked, "Will you adopt me?"

/104/   Duana Linville-Dralus didn't hesitate. Her first words to me were, "Sure! Who are you?"

And that, as they say, was the beginning of a beautiful friendship. Duana and I clicked, and she became my mentor. Over the years, she helped me become a better leader, but—far more importantly—**SHE HELPED ME BECOME A BETTER PERSON.**

Helping people was essentially Duana's religion. Before we'd go out for our annual holiday lunch on the Country Club Plaza, Kansas City's famous shopping district, Du would remind me to tuck a few dollar bills into my coat pocket. Why? So I'd be ready to give whenever we walked past a Salvation Army bell ringer.

Isn't that a wonderful idea? Be ready to give. Whether it's a dollar to charity, a kind word to a co-worker, or a smile to a stranger.

If you can help someone, just Du it.

YOU CAN KNIT WHILE YOU SIT.

Posted on Oct. 6, 2008

TOP EIGHT MENTORING TIPS

When I tell people the title of this book, the most common response is, "Oh, yeah! We all need to look up. We're always staring at our phones." Now, that isn't what Lillian had in mind when she encouraged my brother and sister and I to look up. It was the '60s. We didn't carry phones with us. (I'll wait for a moment, while you gasp.)

I do know what Mom would have said, if we had been out with her, and staring at a phone. You know too. So put the phone away as you consider these quick tips:

1. **REMEMBER WHAT YOUR MOTHER SAID.**
   Say please. Say thank you. Keep your promises. Keep your hands to yourself. Courteous, kind colleagues are highly valued—and far too rare in today's stress-for-success business world. Good manners won't slow you down on the way to the top. It only takes a minute to hold an elevator, send a birthday card, or pause for the answer when you ask, "How are you?" Over the course of a career, those minutes will be time well spent. Trust me on this. I'm a mother.

2. **READ WHAT YOU DON'T NEED.**
   If you always read the trades and the business pubs, congratulations. Now, take it up a notch. Look through a magazine that's completely outside your industry. Enjoy Robert Frost poetry online—you can even find places where he reads it to you. Give your creativity the juice with Dr. Seuss. Expand your literary horizons, and oh, the places you'll go ...

3. **TAP THE MAGIC OF THREE.**
   "Lights, camera, action!" "On your mark, get set, go!" "I love you." Series of threes work, in everything from copywriting to design. Try it the next time you write a speech or column: Tell them what you're going to tell them. Tell them. Then tell them what you told them. Think it doesn't matter? Just do it.

4. **TRUST YOURSELF.**
If your guts tell you something is wrong, listen.

5. **REALIZE THAT YOU ARE REPLACEABLE.**
Now, most people will tell you that you're replaceable at work, but not at home. It's a lovely concept, but look around. Check out the ever-climbing divorce rate. Consider how many parents see their kids every other weekend. Then, decide what you truly value, and make sure your actions reflect your priorities. And, when it comes to being replaced at work, remember: It's easier for the boss to promote you if she knows your replacement is trained and ready to go.

6. **KNOW WHEN TO GO.**
As James Taylor says, "Time may be money, but your money won't buy time." No matter how long it is, life is way too short to spend the majority of your waking hours someplace you don't enjoy. If you're not having fun at work, find something else to do or somewhere else to do it. I know that's easier said than done. But you tell me: How easy is it to get up every morning and go to a job you hate?

7. **IT'S NOT BRAIN SURGERY.**
God love 'em. I don't know what neurosurgeons say. But most jobs are not brain surgery, as my friend Vanessa periodically reminds me. (Many don't even appear to require much grey matter.) Remember, your mistakes aren't life and death issues, even if they feel like it at the time. Take responsibility, fix what you can, learn what you should, and move on.

8. **FORGET WHAT YOUR MOTHER SAID.**
There is such a thing as a stupid question. You don't have to wait to be invited. And if you don't have anything nice to say, call me. We'll do lunch.

CAN YOU SEE ME NOW?

We can draw tremendous creative energy from the people around us if —and this is a big if—we're really aware of the people around us.

**CONSIDER ONE PERSON
YOU SPEND SIGNIFICANT TIME WITH:
IT COULD BE A COLLEAGUE, A KID, OR A LOVER.
FOR THE SAKE OF THIS EXERCISE,
IT DOESN'T MATTER.**

**NOW, THINK ABOUT
YOUR LAST CONVERSATION WITH THAT PERSON.**

Were you distracted by driving, cooking, playing on the computer?

ADD THIS TO THE EQUATION:

How often during that conversation did you make—and hold— direct eye contact?

We all want to be seen.

We want to be heard.

Take the first step.

See and hear someone. *today*.

Posted on Dec. 9, 2008

SAY IT ONCE

Some 30 years ago, before she became my mother-in-law, Betty Harness thought I was about to do something wrong. Flat-out wrong. And this dear, direct, and perceptive woman wasn't going to let that silently go by.

Instead, she said we needed to talk. Immediately. And then:

1. She made sure we were alone for the conversation.

2. She assured me it wasn't me she disapproved of—it was my decision she didn't support.

3. She told me it was important that I understood how she felt, and that she'd never mention it again.

/109/

4. **SHE NEVER MENTIONED IT AGAIN.**

Betty Harness would have been 95 today. I miss her honesty, her sparkle, and her Southern hospitality.

As the saying goes,

"In love we are remembered, and in memories we live."

YOUR LIFE, YOUR LEGACY

HOW WOULD YOU LIKE TO BE REMEMBERED?

Think about it for a bit.

Do you want people to remember you as a kind person
who gently but firmly spoke her mind?

As the father who always had time to shoot hoops?

As a talented artist, big-hearted baker, generous friend?

/110/

_____

or

_____

or

_____

Got your idea in mind? Terrific!

NOW,
WHAT ARE YOU DOING TO MAKE IT HAPPEN?

Posted on April 16, 2009

HOW DO YOU DEFINE...

How do you define winning?

When my sister Eva and I go to the casinos, we consider it a "win" if we put nine pennies into a slot machine and get five pennies back.

WE WON 5 CENTS! YES!

Think that's a goofy definition of winning? Chances are, you're right. However, with our definition on the table, you now have a deeper understanding of me and Eva and how we approach a night out. (You should also know that if we put nine pennies in and get 109 pennies back, the reaction involves enough knee-slapping, hooting, and hollering that any real gamblers sitting nearby typically shake their heads, laugh, and/or move away.)

/111/

Chuckle at our definition of winning, if you want. But the concept is serious:

People aren't dictionaries. We all define things differently — from infidelity to creativity to love.

The next time you're having trouble communicating, don't gamble.

Ask the question: **HOW DO YOU DEFINE...?**

**BEAUTIFUL PEOPLE
RARELY PHOTOGRAPH WELL.**

Posted on May 26, 2009

THE **PERFECT MISTAKE**

I was cleaning out old emails, and found this note from a friend ... sent when I was in the midst of a crisis:

LOVE YOU
AND CALL ME IF YOU NEED FOREVER.

She meant to write, "... if you need anything." But her mistake is perfect, and said exactly what she truly meant.

Mistakes can be marvelous.

By the by, the crisis is long gone. Her love remains.

/113/

THE **LAST TIME**

READY TO GET THOSE
CREATIVE MUSCLES IN SHAPE?

It's best to get out a clean sheet of paper for this one.

Write

" The last time I saw you... "

at the top of the page.

Now, finish the sentence. Then, write five more sentences. You can make this a poem for a parent, a note to an old friend, a prayer for your first love. Whatever you want.

When you're done, burn it.

Or mail it.

You're creative. You'll know which way to go.

Posted on Sept. 14, 2009

FILL 'ER UP!

Recently, I was making plans to visit a friend who has been ill. I called her, and started the conversation by explaining I'd been to a parade to watch my daughter Mary perform with the drill team, I was taking Mary to lunch, I needed to run a few errands, then check on my mom, and take the dog for a walk.

"After that," I said, "I'll be over to see you."

"Your life is full!" she replied.

/115/

One short sentence—and it stopped me short. I've never been a "glass half empty" type of gal, but I wasn't thinking my life was *full*. I was thinking it was freaking insane.

But she's right.

MY LIFE IS FULL.

I'm guessing your life is full too. Wonderfully, astonishingly, temporarily full. It's all a matter of perspective, and I'm changing mine.

Posted on Dec. 14, 2009

THANK YOU FOR YOU

It's good to have friends of all ages. My young buddy Linden brought his dad Chris over to the house this weekend. Our time together reminded me that a preschooler like Linden is the best creativity boost on the planet.

Lessons from Linden:

- If the rules of the game aren't working for you, change the rules.

- When you win, celebrate. When someone else wins, celebrate.

- Be honest. If you don't like the potato pancake, don't eat it.

- Push the limits. How else will you know where they are?

- Believe in your own magic.

- **LAUGH OUT LOUD. SING EVEN LOUDER.**

I'll leave you with one more Lindenism: As they were leaving, Chris reminded his sweet little boy to say "thank you" to Miss Jan.

"Thank you," Linden said.

"Thank you for what?" Chris prompted.

"Thank you for you!"

Thank you for you ☺
Happy day – go play!

Posted on Aug. 23, 2012

YOU'RE NOT INDEBTED.

I'm so glad I started my professional life as a radio reporter. The need to listen carefully so I could quickly capture the best soundbite has helped shape my career—and my relationship to the universe. I hear soundbites others might miss.

FOR EXAMPLE...

One of the speakers on my summertime trip to Jerusalem was a young rebbetzin, a rabbi's wife, who had recently recovered from a critical illness. During the months when she was hospitalized, many people stepped up to help. They fed her family, sat by her bedside, prayed for her recovery.

/117/

Later, she told one of her friends,

"I WILL NEVER BE ABLE TO REPAY ALL THESE KINDNESSES."

The friend quietly replied,

"YOU'RE NOT INDEBTED. YOU'RE CONNECTED."

You're not indebted. You're connected. Could there be a more gracious, freeing, and absolutely accurate way to describe it?

Consider the people you're connected to, and whether it's time you make a face-to-face connection. If so, when it comes to kindness, there's no time like today.

Posted on Nov. 14, 2012

SEE THE MIRACLES

When I was growing up, my family attended Beth Shalom synagogue in Kansas City. Throughout my childhood, we had one religious leader: Rabbi Morris Margolies. The rabbi literally towers over my memories—I can still see him standing in front of the congregation, leading us in worship.

I can still hear him reading a prayer that began, "I am the Lord your God ..."

I can still remember wondering if he meant it literally. Keep in mind: I was 5. And Rabbi Margolies was a force.

He's gone now, but in honor of his impact on my life, I want to share one favorite line from this brilliant, opinionated, outspoken rabbi:

"THE PARTING OF THE RED SEA IS NO GREATER MIRACLE THAN THE SEA ITSELF."

May his memory be a blessing. And may we all see the miracles that surround us, every day.

Posted on Feb. 22, 2013

GOOD USE OF YOUR TIME

I take yoga classes at a rec center—the yoga room is right next to the big gym. Every Tuesday night after class, I walk by all the adults sitting outside the gym while the adorable little children practice gymnastics.

The kids are a hoot. They're tumbling and balancing and falling and leaping and laughing. I know this, because there are huge windows so people can watch the action from the waiting room.

Unfortunately, the windows aren't all that necessary.

As I left the other night, I noticed that—as usual—almost all the adults were focused on their iPads, cellphones and laptop computers. Only a few /119/ were watching the kids. One of the other yoga participants, walking next to me, said, "Isn't that great? Everyone is making such good use of their time!"

We were leaving yoga. It wasn't the time to go ballistic. This is.

Ignoring a 6-year-old on the balance beam is not a good use of your time. Missing your third-grader do a perfect dismount is not a good use of your time. Playing solitaire online when a child is right in front of you doing a cartwheel is not a good use of your time.

And it's not only an adult-kid thing. We're in danger of losing eye contact, people. Remember eye contact? That thing you used to make with another human being before we turned our focus to all things electronic?

Listen up, because I'm ranting and I'm right: **YOU DON'T GET THIS DAY AGAIN. ONLY TODAY. ONLY TODAY.**

LOOK UP.

IF YOU'RE LOOKING FOR SYMPATHY,
IT'S IN THE DICTIONARY
BETWEEN SHIT AND SYPHILIS.

Posted on March 9, 2015

KEEP WALKING

Harrison Ford's plane crash last week reminded me of one of my all-time favorite sayings:

ANY LANDING YOU WALK AWAY FROM IS A GOOD LANDING.

Thanks to Earl, the WWII pilot who gave me that advice, I've felt much better about any number of crashes, including heart-rending relationships, broken trusts, and disappointing business deals. I've also used the line as reassurance after a dangerously stupid lane change at 70 miles per hour.

/121/

Ah, I can hear your brain coming up with similar situations. At one time or another, we've all been there.

Say it with me, dear heart:

Any landing you walk away from
is a good landing.

SHUMWAY'S LAW

I stumbled across Shumway's Law years ago, while reading a magazine article about heart transplant surgeon Norman Shumway.

The law is perfection:

THE **BLEEDING** ALWAYS STOPS.

Wouldn't that be a great line for a poem? I'll give you an exercise option here, and you're welcome to do both.

1. Use "The bleeding always stops" as the title of a poem, and include it somewhere within the poem.

_____

_____

_____

_____

2. Write your own law.

_____

_____

_____

Posted March 24, 2015

SONS OF BITCHES

GRIEF IS SNEAKY.
IT'S STARTLING.
IT SIDLES UP AND GRABS YOU,
UNAWARES.

Grief hit this morning, when I was sitting at the dining room table, having my morning coffee and reading the comics online. I got to Zen Pencils, alphabetically last on my organized list, and was slammed by the end panel, featuring a quote from astronaut Edgar Mitchell. In the comic, he was standing on the moon with the world's political leaders, pointing at /123/ the blue marble Earth and saying:

"LOOK AT THAT, YOU SON OF A BITCH."

Maybe it was the quote. Maybe it was reading the quote while drinking my coffee. But I was instantly transported to a chair in the corner of Mrs. Dougherty's apartment in Florida.

Joyce Dougherty was (and it still feels wrong to use the past tense when talking about her) my *bestfriendinthewholeworldsincefourthgrade* Lynn's mom. At some point in our decades together, I started calling her Mom, but I typically called her Mrs. Dougherty and that's still how I think of her.

Lynn and her hubby Paul had a mother-in-law suite in their house for Mrs. Dougherty. When I'd go visit, I typically got up before Lynn and would go over to have coffee with Mrs. Dougherty.

We had our places. She'd sit in her corner chair. I'd sit in my corner chair. And, as we enjoyed our coffee and read the paper, she would share her opinions on what she was reading and what she was thinking. She was a woman of strong opinions on everything from Lynn to life to politics to people to me and my daughters.

And, when her opinion was negative—let's say we were discussing politicians—one of her favorite phrases was, *sons of bitches.*

I can still hear her saying it.

ISN'T IT FUNNY HOW YOU CAN HEAR PEOPLE LONG AFTER THEY'RE GONE, IF YOU THINK OF THE RIGHT PHRASE?

I can hear Dad tell Mom dinner was fine. "How was dinner, Allen?" "It was fine." Took me years to realize that he meant exactly that; it always sounded negative to me at the time.

Dad meant *it was fine.*

Mrs. Dougherty meant they were *sons of bitches.*

SHE WAS ALWAYS RIGHT. THEY WERE.

Mrs. Dougherty was a mother, grandmother, friend, artist, cook. She was incredibly well read. She was amazingly talented. Her eyes sparkled. She had style—she could wear a cape and a beret and make it work. That's no easy feat.

Mrs. Dougherty missed nothing.

She lived and loved wholeheartedly.

She was equally at ease with old people and young children.

She was the contradiction we all are:
painfully direct one moment, kind and giving the next.

I always felt that part of the gift of being Lynn's best friend was being included in Mrs. Dougherty's circle of love.

Mrs. Dougherty was a tiny woman physically—shorter than I am by /125/ the end, if you can imagine that. Much thinner. But she gave meaning to Shakespeare's phrase, "Though she be but little, she is fierce."

GRIEF IS FIERCE.
LOSS IS FIERCE.
THEY ARE EMOTIONAL SONS OF BITCHES.

This morning's sneak attack reminded me of how even a quick memory of someone we love can bring unexpected tears and a palpable ache.

And isn't that wonderful?

The people we love stay with us, forever.

They are part of who we are, who we will be.

I am who I am because of Mrs. Dougherty and Dad and others.

LOVED, BUT NEVER LOST.

S.O.B.

I told him

he was a

good for nothing

son of a bitch

and I meant

every word but

every word was a lie.

His mother was really

a lovely person

and he was very good

at some things.

Very good,

if you know what I mean.

And you know what I mean

because we've all been there.

We've all been in love

with a good for nothing

son of a bitch

and the horse

that he rode in on.

**HE CAN GET GLAD
IN THE SAME PANTS HE GOT MAD IN.**

Posted on Jan. 22, 2015

THE **AMAZING GRACE** OF **OK**

I don't usually remember dates, but I remember this one: On Dec. 23, 2014, I got the flu. We're talking nasty bug. I don't know what my temperature was—I'm guessing 102 or 103. We didn't have a working thermometer in the house. (Yes. You're right. One more reason I won't be named Mom of the Year.)

I crawled into bed wearing long underwear, a sweatshirt, flannel pajamas, and wool socks, and buried myself under three blankets and a comforter. I was still cold. It wasn't good. The next day was worse. It wasn't a stomach flu. I coughed. I ached. I froze. There were many days during the next few weeks where showering was an accomplishment. First of all, I had to get out of bed or off the couch. I had to take off five layers of clothes. And then I had to stand in the shower, and standing for more than a minute took a lot of energy.

I'm not making this up. Ask my family.

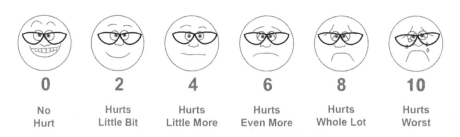

0	2	4	6	8	10
No Hurt	Hurts Little Bit	Hurts Little More	Hurts Even More	Hurts Whole Lot	Hurts Worst

After a while, I began having serious trouble breathing, and finally went to the doctor. The flu had morphed into bronchitis; she prescribed antibiotics and an inhaler. Not long after that, I started feeling human.

Then, one wonderful day, I woke up with enough energy to be me again. The living dead had rejoined the living. I was grateful for everything. The ease of climbing the stairs. My appetite. A good deep breath. If you've never had asthma, let me assure you:

THERE IS NOTHING BETTER THAN BREATHING.

A funny thing happened a few days later, though.

I wasn't consumed with gratitude for the amazing grace of simply feeling OK. Apparently it's easy to take breathing for granted when you're fully oxygenated.

We are people of short memories. Most of us have faced illnesses or accidents that limit our day-to-day activities. We fall, we break, we need help to take a shower or make lunch or pull up our pants. Then, if we're lucky, we heal.

Two seconds later, we forget. We forget how awful it was to be ill or broken. We forget how it felt to be needy.

We forget how fabulous it is to be whole.

The flu has flown, thank God. Or chicken soup. Or amoxicillin. I want to wrap the feeling of gratitude around me, a while longer.

Posted on March 5, 2015

MY AMERICAN SNIPER

I went to the doctor yesterday for my annual physical, which included a blood test. I'm a talker (you never noticed?) so naturally I had a conversation with the guy who was drawing blood:

JAN: I've had a million blood tests. I never look.

GUY WITH NEEDLE: Neither do I.

JAN: Ha!

GUY: Seriously. I've been doing this for years. I don't look. I feel for the vein. And I tell the technicians I'm training, they shouldn't look either. Looking is just a distraction.

/130/

Isn't that fascinating? Looking for the vein distracts him from finding the vein.

And that makes me wonder ... what are you and I looking for that's just a distraction? Are there steps we take, every day, that really aren't necessary? What could we do—possibly better—if we focused on the end goal, rather than the first step?

As you ponder that, let me address the immediate distraction: What does this post have to do with an American sniper? In chatting with the technician, I found out he spent 30 years in the Green Berets as a sniper.

EVERYBODY HAS A STORY, MY FRIEND. EVERYBODY.

By the by, he got the needle in my vein on the first try. No pain. No bruise. No looking.

WELCOME HOME

During one of my recent whines about leaving Florida sunshine for Kansas cold, my friend Steve sent me this simple message:

COLD WELCOMES YOU HOME.

Isn't that a fabulous phrase? Almost made me feel better about getting on the plane. Almost.

Your exercise for today? Take 45 seconds and come up with five words that could fill in the blank:

/131/

_____ welcomes you home.

_____ welcomes you home.

_____ welcomes you home.

_____ welcomes you home.

_____ welcomes you home.

Posted on Feb. 1, 2017

WHAT WOULD **DU** DO?

I know what Du would do if she read that headline.

She'd laugh.

Duana Linville-Dralus had the best laugh. She was a completely irresistible, throw-your-head-back-and-roar kind of woman—one of the best people who ever walked this planet. She was my mentor, which makes me one of the luckiest people who ever walked this planet.

Feb. 1 was Du's birthday, so today is the perfect time for me to cherish the memory of that laugh, and share three of my favorite answers to the question I still ask myself: "What would Du do?"

- **IF YOU CAN HELP SOMEONE, HELP THEM.** Whether or not they can help you in return is completely immaterial. Du helped me before she knew who I was or what I did. I was just a young woman in serious need of assistance.

- **BE TRUE TO YOURSELF.** Du was the first woman leader I knew who was wholeheartedly who she was all the time. She wasn't a different person in the boardroom than she was in her kitchen.

- **DO SOMETHING NICE EVERY DAY.** One of the kind things Du did was simple but powerful: She kept money in her pocket. That way, she was already ready to give to people in need.

/133/

When Duana's cancer came back full force, people would periodically ask her, "Are you going to die?" (True story. I was there when it happened. Several times.) Her response was always the same: "Yep! But not today. Not today. So let's do something!"

Today, here's what I'm going to do. I'm going to open the bottle of champagne I keep in the fridge, because she believed in always being ready for a celebration. I'm going to toast Duana's children, Deb and Doug, for sharing their mom with me. I'm going to toast Maureen and the rest of our group, for being part of an amazing sisterhood. And I'm going to toast Duana, a remarkable woman whose memory is now, and shall always be, a blessing.

Posted on May 1, 2018

THE **PROBLEM** WITH **DEAD PEOPLE**

Writers don't typically give you the punch line to a story in the lead paragraph. We want you to have a reason to keep reading. Nonetheless, I'm going to clarify the problem with dead people right now:

THEY CAN'T APOLOGIZE.

Ah, now you know. And you're still here, aren't you? I get it. Your dead person can't apologize. Neither can mine.

The good news? We can still forgive them and move on.

Have you seen *Coco*? No, I'm not digressing. The movie beautifully illustrates the Day of the Dead concept. To loosely summarize: Our loved ones aren't truly gone as long as we remember them. I want to take that theory to the next step—let's say the ones who hurt us in life aren't truly at peace until we forgive them.

Sure, they had power here. Your dead one might have crushed your self-esteem or changed your perspective on life. But they're gone now, and we have the power. We can stop letting their past actions determine our future. We can let them rest in peace, as we move forward in peace.

STEP ONE: **RECLAIM YOUR POWER.**

In my *Creative Chai* e-book, I talk about wizards: We grant some people (living or dead) the power to change how we see ourselves. Every time your mind goes to that negative place, with that negative interaction, visualize a stop sign. See it clearly in your head. Then, stop the voice and force yourself to think of something else. I've done it, and you can too—I know you can.

STEP TWO : HEAR ME.

If you have trouble stopping the voice and mentally turning the corner, substitute my voice. Hear me saying, "You are amazing and good and strong." Because you are. If you can't hear me in your head, then visualize this:

I AM AMAZING
AND GOOD
AND STRONG.

If that seems like a leap, try the affirmation I use:

I CHOOSE TO BE KIND TO MYSELF.

/135/

STEP THREE : GRANT FORGIVENESS,
FOR YOUR OWN SAKE.

This step is the big one, and we all have different ways to forgive. Maybe you write the issue down on paper and burn the paper. Maybe you say, aloud, "I forgive you." Maybe you say, "What you did was horrible and wrong; I love you still. I thank you for all the good you did, and I forgive you."

STEP FOUR : UNDERSTAND
THAT IT'S A PROCESS.

Be kind to yourself. If you've been carrying a dead person on your back for years, that's a lot of weight. You might not drop it all today. But you can let it go! You can. Because you, my friend, are far stronger than you know.

FORGIVE AND ...

I used to think I was absolutely no good at the whole forgive and forget concept. Oh, sure. I'd forgive. But I'd never, ever, ever forget.

Funny thing though. As it turns out, once I forgave, I began to forget. Automatically. Is that how it works with you? At some point, you turn around and realize: It's gone. The anger, the hurt. Whatever. It's gone.

IN ITS PLACE?

More room for laughter.

For wonder.

For creativity.

More room for you.

Give it a try.

Forgive someone.

See what you get in return.

BREATHE IN. BREATHE OUT.

1-24-92, FOR HAROLD

grief
with its own
rhymeless reasonless rhythm
taps

and you answer the questions quietly.
this should be in the eulogy;
this goes in the paper.

grief taps
and you face a room full of caskets,
a variety of vaults.

We're dust to dust. It doesn't matter.

grief
taps

and graveside you stand dry-eyed
saying kaddish for the living.

grief taps
as you shovel dirt on the chosen casket.

Taps play.

And you'll cry later,
leaning on your shovel in the garden.

Posted on Feb. 18, 2019

SORRY ꜰᴏʀ YOUR LOST

First things first: The title is not a typo. Amid all the "sorry for your loss" messages I received after Mom died in November, I got one text that read, "Sorry for your lost." The friend who sent that speaks English as her second language, so I don't know if it was a typo or exactly the word she wanted.

Either way, it's perfect. "Sorry for your lost" made me feel better.

Now, my reaction to that text is random and reflects my life as a word nerd. However, after a few months of mourning Mom, I've discovered some (possibly) universal, creative ways to help people we care about through tough times, whether they are mourning the loss of a person, pet, job, or relationship.

/139/

Grief is, of course, incredibly personal—and different each time. A friend might react differently to the death of his father than his mother. One person might see divorce as a *Hallelujah!* moment, while the other spouse is heartbroken.

THERE IS NO ONE SIZE FITS ALL ANSWER.
THERE IS NO "SOLUTION."

YOU WON'T "FIX" LIFE FOR A GRIEVING FRIEND.
BUT YOU SURE CAN HELP...

Posted on Feb. 18, 2019

HOW TO HELP A GRIEVING FRIEND

SHOW UP

Let's start with a question: Is the grieving friend a Facebook friend or a face-to-face friend? If we're talking high school pal you haven't seen in 30 years, then a heartfelt comment on Facebook is fine. If it's possible to add a personal note ("I loved going to your house after school because your mom always made me feel so welcome."), that's tremendously comforting.

/140/

If the grieving friend is a colleague, relative, coffee buddy, book club buddy, faith-group buddy, etc., posting online, even with a personal note, is not sufficient. Change your plans and attend the memorial service. It may be cold and inconvenient and you don't want to be there. Keep in mind, your friend doesn't want to be there either. Can't attend? Make a donation. Send flowers. Do something that says, "I share your pain."

One friend, knowing I love the E. E. Cummings poem, "i carry your heart with me (i carry it in my heart)" sent flowers with the note: "I carry your heart and your sorrow." I will treasure that note forever.

If you're not sure what to do, consider what this friend has done for you in the past. If she sent a sweet card with a handwritten note after your pet passed away, send her a sweet card with a handwritten note. If he sent a funny card to cheer you up after you got fired, send him a funny card to cheer him up after his partner walks out.

And, in these days of social media, remember the power of a phone call. I know it's hard. But you can do it. Remember: It's not about you. It's about your friend. She'll remember the call long after she has forgotten the conversation.

ASK THE RIGHT QUESTION

When you call, let the grieving friend talk. If you feel awkward, try this: Rather than asking your friend, "How are you doing?" ask, "How are you doing today?" As noted in *Option B*, Sheryl Sandberg and Adam Grant's book on grief, that one simple word changes everything. "How are you doing?" prompts the automatic, "Fine. I'm fine. Thank you for asking." "How are you doing today?" opens the door to honest conversation.

"How are you doing today?" also reflects the reality of grief. During the course of a month, a week, a day, an hour, how I feel changes. Maybe you're calling right after I've opened a drawer and seen a note Mom wrote to me 18 years ago, a note I saved because it was dear.

/141/

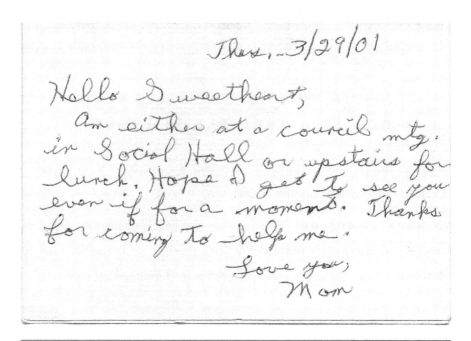

I'm missing Mom so much at that moment that it's a physical pain. But maybe you're calling after I wrapped up a big client assignment and feel like I knocked it out of the ballpark. I'm not thinking about Mom at all. After the initial tsunami, grief is not a constant flood of emotions. It's an ebb and flow.

Of course, not knowing what mood you'll be dealing with can make picking up the phone even more daunting. I get it. This works for just about any grieving situation, any mood: "Hi! I was thinking about you and wanted to check in. How are you doing today?"

WARNING: Try to avoid clichés that really don't help. "I know exactly how you feel," is never an accurate statement. And, while you may believe, "It's all God's plan," your friend—even if deeply religious—may not find that comforting. As a favorite card from Emily McDowell & Friends says:

"IF THIS IS GOD'S PLAN, GOD IS A TERRIBLE PLANNER."

When in doubt, listen. Remember the call doesn't have to be lengthy; it's the thought and effort that count.

TO WRAP THINGS UP: "Good to talk with you." lets people know they weren't a burden as they unburdened their grief. If you're nearby, take the phone call to the next step: "Want to grab some lunch next week?"

PROVIDE FOOD

I know, I know. Everyone's on a diet. It doesn't matter. Everyone has to eat. And grief doesn't lend itself to menu planning, grocery shopping, cooking, cleaning, etc. Unless your friend, and your friend's family, is on such a strict eating plan that food would be an irritation, bring food. Send food. Take him to lunch.

If you love to cook or bake, homemade food is wonderful—one of the most comforting moments in my grieving process was when a friend brought an entire Italian feast to the house, including pasta made with her grandmother's old recipe. The food was delicious, and we felt the love from my friend and her grandmother.

/143/

BONUS: **TALKING ABOUT THE FOOD** OPENED THE **FLOODGATES** OF **CONVERSATION.**

But don't feel like you need to bring homemade goodies—or stick around for the meal. Some people prefer privacy. Some friends prefer not to stay. All good. Buy a roasted chicken at the store, bag o'salad, and a baguette. Drop it off, give a hug, and go.

Out of town? Send food.

We received several baskets of goodies, and they were wonderful. They not only kept us fed, but they made us feel loved.

SHOW UP AGAIN

While the ebb and flow of grief never ends, the first year can be horrifically hard, especially when the grief involves a death. All those firsts. First birthday without him. First anniversary without her. First Thanksgiving. And on and on and on.

Grief is also isolating. Something that helped identify you—a person, a professional position, a pet—is no longer here. As my sister told me recently, **"IT'S TIME TO FIND A NEW NORMAL."**

True friends are the GPS on that path. One dear friend, who lives in another state, mails little notes to me on a regular basis, with a handwritten message like: "Thinking about you and hoping it's a good week!" The real message, of course, goes far beyond that. Every note tells me that I am in her heart. I am in her thoughts and prayers. I am not forgotten; my loss is acknowledged and remembered—even when the words on the paper say nothing about that. Each note is a gift.

Another friend called recently and left a voicemail: "It's been a little while since your mom died, and I'm just thinking about you and wondering if the world feels a little less shaken."

She left the message while stuck in traffic on her commute home. The voicemail lasted 27 seconds. Not a huge time commitment, my friends. And yet, by showing up again, she told me that I matter to her. That my mother matters. That my grief matters. Now, that's huge.

CONSOLE BETTER

Years ago, I wrote a post titled "Dance Better." What the past few months have taught me is that I need to console better. Being a baker, I typically bring food to grieving friends, but too often I've taken a "one and done" approach. In the future, I'll do better.

And, unfortunately, I'll have the opportunity. We all will:

LOSS IS AN INEVITABLE PART OF LOVE.

To everyone who has helped me these past few months, *thank you* doesn't /145/ begin to cover it. I do carry your heart, and I am blessed that you carry mine.

I carry your heart and your sorrow.
xoxo
Cheri

CHANGING STONES AT MY FATHER'S GRAVE

The pebble I left last time,
Gravel picked up near your grave,
Is not a fitting tribute.

Today I bring a tumbled tiger eye,
Gleaming with golden stripes.
A stone of undeniable substance.

Like everything perfect, it is flawed.
A rough crack resisted the tumbler.
A break distorts the shining lines.

Like everything lost, you remain.
I hold your beauty and your fury,
Flares of pipe dreams and sweet tobacco.

Today, Sheffield Cemetery is silent.
No wind, no visitors,
no burials.

There is only you in the grave,
And your daughter,
offering a stone.

NOTE : It is a Jewish tradition to leave stones, rather than flowers. After my father died, I began bringing polished stones to his grave, to honor the tradition while still leaving something beautiful as a tribute. Ask five Jews for the reason behind the stones, and you'll get five different answers. (Because. Judaism. Many questions. Many answers.) I like the idea that while flowers and people die, stones and memories remain.

CHAPTER SIX:

LESSONS FROM MY DAUGHTERS

ARE YOU HAPPY OF ME?

Since I began *Look Up* with a chapter about my mom, it's only fitting that I wrap it up with stories about my daughters, Kate and Mary.

Katherine Sophia and Mary Nell are the reason you're holding this book; I started it as a paperback reminder for them of what I value in life. A literary legacy, if you will. Blog posts—even 1,300 of them—felt too ephemeral. I wanted something solid.

Over the years, the girls have inspired, and tolerated, innumerable blog posts. They've given me the perfect platform for promoting the creative building blocks of determination, honesty, persistence, humor—the list goes on and on.

Parents, naturally, tend to think their children are creative geniuses. Parents, naturally, are right. As Picasso famously said,

"EVERY CHILD IS AN ARTIST. THE PROBLEM IS HOW TO REMAIN AN ARTIST ONCE WE GROW UP."

Growing up is scary. It doesn't take long (First grade? Second grade?) before other people's opinions matter. A lot. We start looking at ourselves through the eyes of others. And then we change our beautiful selves to fit in.

How can you remain an artist? By appreciating your unique talents. By daring to be—and share—your best, true self. By finding the courage to leap into new adventures, fully aware that you might stumble. You might fall.

You remain an artist by embracing what children inherently know. We all stumble. We all fall.

THE ARTISTS GET UP AGAIN, LEAP AGAIN, AND SOAR.

Posted on March 6, 2008

WHEN YOU FALL ...

My 14-year-old daughter Mary tried out for the high school drill team Wednesday night. She's been on the junior high team, was comfortable with the tryout routine, and knew exactly what she needed to do.

WHEN HER TIME IN THE SPOTLIGHT CAME, ## SHE SMILED, SHE DANCED, SHE LEAPED.

THEN, UNFORTUNATELY, ## SHE FELL.

/149/

Her heart fell, too. But you know what she did? She kept on smiling, got right back up, and gave it her best. She didn't cry until the dance was over and she was out of the auditorium.

We could all learn a lesson from Mary. When we take a leap, sometimes we soar. Sometimes we fall. The trick is finding the courage to get up and do it again—and the determination to do it better.

Mary did two more leaps before the dance was done. Beautifully. I'm proud to say: She made the team.

UPDATE: Mary's decision to get back up made all the difference. She went on to become a team officer for the nationally recognized, award-winning Olathe South Golden Girls. Every moment contains amazing possibilities.

NO APOLOGIES

The next time you take a creative leap—let's say you try writing a haiku or cooking a new recipe—don't apologize before presenting your work.

You know exactly what I mean.

"I'm sorry this is ..."

"I was going to (blah blah blah), but (more blah blah blah). Sorry!"

Those apologies aren't only unnecessary, they're dangerous. They make the people who are about to read the poem or eat the soufflé doubt the quality of the pending experience.

Instead, set yourself up for success. Take this advice offered during a summer session class I took at the Iowa Writers' Workshop. When any of us would start making excuses before reading a poem, the instructor would say,

"STOP.

**ALL YOU NEED TO SAY IS,
'THIS IS FAIRLY NEW
AND IT SMACKS OF BRILLIANCE.'"**

Posted on May 1, 2008

BREAK THE RULES

Like most little kids, my daughter Kate loved coloring books. She'd scribble all over them, and I'd applaud her brilliance.

Then, one horrific day, she started drawing inside the lines.

I was distraught. My free-spirited child had been compromised by society's creativity-snuffing rules and regulations.

For consolation, I turned to an artist friend, Nancy, a good and gentle soul.

"Jan," she said quietly, "It's fine. It's all part of the process. Kate has to learn to draw inside the lines, so she can *choose* to draw outside the lines."

/151/

You know the rules.
What's your choice?

Posted on June 16, 2008

DRIVING LESSONS

In Kansas, kids can start driving, legally, at the ripe old age of 14. This made sense when the law was enacted and Kansas was one big farm and the vehicles were tractors. It makes less sense now, but ...

I'm teaching 14-year-old Mary to drive. Watching her behind the wheel reminds me of an essential creativity tip:

FOCUS ON WHERE YOU'RE GOING.
IF YOU'RE MOVING AHEAD, LOOK AHEAD.
IF YOU'RE BACKING UP, LOOK BACK.

/152/

And if someone starts talking, don't look at them until the car is stopped. *Even if it's your mother. And even if she's screaming.*

LESSONS FROM THE **FOURTH GRADE**

In my attempt to turn our recent basement flood into a positive, I've been using the resulting disarray as incentive to clean things up. And I found this note among the girls' school papers. I can't tell you if it belonged to Kate or Mary, but I can tell you it was written in fourth grade:

From the author talk today I learned ...

that you never, never, never give up.
And don't ~~through~~ away your first draft.
      throw

/153/

HELPING MY DAUGHTER

WITH HER TERM PAPER ON DANTE

Abandon all hope ye who enter here

FIRST CIRCLE

I pull my yellowed copy of *The Divine Comedy* off the shelf.
She sneers. All she needs is Google.
Clearly, I'm in the wrong concentric room.
Souls in limbo are not actively punished.

SECOND CIRCLE

She absolutely, positively will not discuss lust with me.
Instead, she reads her notes, dictates and whines,
trapped with me, seemingly forever.

THIRD CIRCLE

Twenty agonizing minutes later, I ask,
"What circle of hell are *we* in?"
She doesn't laugh. She is 16. I am 50.
There is nothing divine or comedic here.
Is every parent a glutton for punishment?

FOURTH CIRCLE

I continue hoarding my knowledge,
she continues wasting our time.
We strain against giant weights
and charge at each other.

FIFTH CIRCLE

The wrathful fight in the river Styx,
while the sullen are trapped beneath the water.
I wonder how many children Dante had.

SIXTH CIRCLE

We continue our descent through hell.

Or are we ascending?

I can't remember, she doesn't care.

The heretics are burning.

SEVENTH CIRCLE

The sky rains fire on people violent against art.

Their suicidal neighbors hang from thorny, blackened trees.

I shudder, and pick up the book.

"Just put it down," she says. "Holy crap."

/155/

EIGHTH CIRCLE

As ditches fill with the knowingly evil, my daughter writhes on the floor.

"Turnitin.com will say this is plagiarized.

I'm gonna flunk. I'm gonna die."

Since flatterers are steeped in excrement,

I have no encouragement to offer.

NINTH CIRCLE

Our journey takes us to the end of body copy, paragraph 1.

Satan is waiting, his three heads chewing on each other.

He wants to escape. I sympathize.

But, Heaven help us, Purgatory and paragraph 2 are waiting.

Helping My Daughter with Her Term Paper on Dante was included in the book *From the Heart: A Collection of Stories and Poems from the Front Lines of Parenting*, published in 2010.

Posted on Nov. 13, 2008

ARE YOU HAPPY OF ME?

When my youngest daughter was a toddler, she made up wonderful phrases and words. For example, when caught in the act of misbehaving—a daily event—Mary would simply stop, look up at me with her big brown eyes, and ask, "Are you happy of me, Mommy?"

How can you not be happy of someone creative enough to come up with that line?

Another common Mary phrase was,

"I DID THAT LASTERDAY."

Lasterday could be yesterday, or the day before, or the day before that. It covered a fair amount of territory, but I always knew exactly what she meant. She'd been there and done that. Lasterday.

Don't settle for the ordinary. Don't accept, "It is what it is." Make it what it should be. Do that, and I'll be happy of you. Far more importantly, *you'll* be happy of you. Lasterday, today, and tomorrow.

Posted on Dec. 10, 2009

RECOGNIZE THE RAT

Every year, I have my daughter Mary address holiday cards. We get them in the mail the day after Thanksgiving. Like clockwork.

This year, I'm running so fast in so many directions, I forgot. I have the cards; they're lovely. But I don't want to send them now. Why?

BECAUSE I'M NOT THE FIRST
TO GET MY HOLIDAY CARDS IN THE MAIL.

Yes. That's right. I have turned seasonal greetings of love and joy, /157/ friendship and good wishes, into a competition. I turn everything into a competition. It's not good. It's bad. Real bad.

It's also possible I'm not the only one doing this. I'm guessing, of course. But I can hear you laughing, and I don't *think* you're laughing only at me.

We need to recognize how this became a rat race, folks. And then we need to do something about it. I, for one, am ready to stop being the rat.

After all, as journalist Mary Schmich said in one of my favorite essays,

"THE RACE IS LONG
AND, IN THE END,
IT'S ONLY WITH YOURSELF."

Posted on Jan. 11, 2010

QUESTION "NORMAL"

Yesterday, my daughter Kate and I went for a drive, and we both remarked about how hot it was. The thermometer registered 24 degrees.

Now, 24 degrees is not a heatwave. But, here in the Midwest, we've gotten used to single-digit temperatures and below-zero wind chills. Sunshine and 24 felt absolutely tropical.

SUNSHINE AND 24 IS NOT TROPICAL.

It's interesting how quickly we adjust to adverse situations—and I'm not just talking cold weather. Look at your home, your office, your relationships. What have you accepted as normal that isn't?

FOR EXAMPLE: Did you say you'd paint the foundation of your home to match the siding 20 years ago? Is it still a different color? (Yes. Yes. Light blue foundation and grey siding—and I don't even notice it anymore.)

It's a new year. Take a good look around, question the norm, and go for better. Expecting more is the first step toward getting more.

IF YOU BUILD IT, THEY WILL READ

Want to take a fresh look at a familiar topic? Compose a concrete poem. In concrete poetry, the words on the page take the shape of the poem's subject. You can write about a house, a coffee cup, an arrow, whatever—pick a shape and go!

ELEANOR DOESN'T WANT TO MOVE

I

have lived

in this house my

whole life. I have had

the same bedroom my whole life.

Except when I was a baby. Then I was in

a bassinet in mom and dad's room. But that doesn't really count.

So this has been my bedroom my whole life. And the

carpet is purple. The new house doesn't have carpet.

If it did, it wouldn't be purple. When we come back

to visit, I want to come back to this house. I'll knock on

the door and tell the   people who live here

that we used to live   here. I will ask them

if I can go up to my   bedroom and see if

the carpet is still purple.

Posted on Aug. 18, 2010

CELEBRATE FIRSTS. AND LASTS.

One of my favorite poems, *Cascando* by Samuel Beckett, includes the phrase, **"THERE IS A LAST EVEN OF LAST TIMES."** Today I am incredibly aware of another truth: This is a last even of first times.

Mary starts her senior year in high school today. Those of you who have loved me for years know what that means ... the annual "first day of school" photo will soon pop up in your email.

LAST TIME, FOLKS. LAST FIRST.

For the rest of you, let me explain. Ever since Kate started kindergarten, Tom and I have been among the millions of parents taking photos on the first day of school. We could have printed the pics, framed them, and called it a day. But where's the fun in that? Instead, I emailed multiple photos to everyone who had ever met the girls, assuming they'd be thrilled.

I mean, heck. We're talking the cutest children ever born. How could you not be thrilled?

For the first few years, including this kindergarten moment, it was only Kate in the photos. Then, Kate and Mary, all decked out with new backpacks and eager to go to class. Those first years, the photo frenzy continued from our house all the way to the elementary school.

Flash forward to junior high. High school. It was harder to get them to pause for the camera. Almost impossible to get them in the same frame.

Then, whoosh! Kate had the audacity to grow up and go off to college—out of reach of even my zoom lens. And, for some reason, she refused to take a photo of herself on the first day of school and email it to me so I could forward it. (Yes. I seriously made that request. I do not let go easily.)

So, for the past few years, it's just been Mary, who may groan and grimace this morning as she runs out to her car, but she will also stop and grin for the camera. Because she's a good kid. And she knows that celebrating firsts, and lasts, is important.

/161/

To all of you who have helped send Kate and Mary off to school for the past 15 years, thank you. You have done more than share our joy. You have doubled it.

GIFTS

If you could give yourself one gift, what would it be?

IT CAN BE MAGICAL, MERCENARY, MYTHICAL...

WHATEVER MAKES YOU HAPPY.

I'd like a camera that takes pictures of the past, so I could have snapshots now of everything I didn't take pictures of then.

/162/

Posted on March 29, 2011

THE BIRD IS DEAD

In honor of my firstborn's 21st birthday today, let me tell you my favorite Kate story.

I was driving Kate home from a visit with the grandparents. She was about 4 or 5, sitting next to me in the front seat of our van.

SUDDENLY, A BIRD FELL DOWN ON THE STREET IN FRONT OF US. SPLAT. DEAD. KAPUT.

I looked at Kate's little face. She looked up at me. I knew I had to say something. I was the mom. She was my kid. I did the best I could.

"I think the bird's OK," I said.

"Mom," Kate said, gently but firmly, "the bird is dead."

And that has become a Harness family classic. You'd be amazed at how often the correct response to a situation is, "Mom, the bird is dead."

Never underestimate your audience. And remember:

YOU CAN FOOL ALL OF THE PEOPLE SOME OF THE TIME AND SOME OF THE PEOPLE ALL OF THE TIME.

BUT DON'T MESS AROUND WITH KATE.

Posted on Jan. 8, 2012

BEST LINE OF THE WEEK

On Saturday, Mary and I enjoyed watching a dress rehearsal by the Olathe South Golden Girls, the drill team she performed with during her high school years. Right after one high-kicking dance, the coach stopped the music, talked to the girls quietly, and sent them back to the dressing room.

She then turned to those of us gathered and said, "I apologize for the delay, but this was a teachable moment. Mistakes are easy to fix. Habits are hard to break."

I don't know what the mistake was.

I do know that's a perfect phrase.

MISTAKES ARE EASY TO FIX.
HABITS ARE HARD TO BREAK.

WHEN IN DOUBT, DON'T.

Posted on June 13, 2012

HELP

How talented are you when it comes to asking for help?

Monday, I was stomping around the house. The dining room and kitchen were crammed with boxes—we had new carpet installed last week and haven't had a chance to unpack, put things away. There were more boxes from Mom's pending move in the entryway. Yet more boxes packed for charity and sitting by the fireplace.

Which stack pushed me over the edge? Doesn't matter. Here's the issue: I still expect people to read my mind. It's the classic, "If you really loved me, you'd know." So, imagine my surprise when Mary said:

"Mom, do you need help with something? All you have to do is ask."

She didn't know that I wanted help to move the boxes. She was trying her best to stay out of my control-freak way. Whoa. I came out of insane mode long enough to say, "Yes. I would really appreciate your help. Would you please move all these boxes up to my office?"

And, snap. Easy as that, boxes disappeared. Take a lesson from John, Paul, George, and Ringo. Get better at asking:

WON'T YOU PLEASE, PLEASE HELP ME?

"SHUT UP." "SAY WHAT?"

When Mary was a little thing, maybe 3 years old, I was rushing to get her and Kate (probably 7 years old at the time) ready to go—Mary to daycare and Kate to school. Mary was being poky. I told her to hurry up. She told me to shut up.

Say what?

"Did **YOU** tell **ME** to shut up?" I asked, pulling myself up to a towering 5 feet in full strict-mother mode.

Picture the panic, as the toddler tried to squirm her way out of /167/ this one. **YOU COULD SEE THE CREATIVE BRAIN CELLS IN ACTION.** Her eyes were literally spinning. Then, she stood up straight to declare her innocence.

"No, momma!" she insisted. "I said, 'Shit!'"

Well, I started laughing so hard I had to leave the room. At which point, poor little Kate came trailing after me to point out that first Mary told me to shut up, then she cursed, and she still didn't get in trouble.

My girls. I'll keep 'em both. :)

Posted on Dec. 6, 2012

GET THE MESSAGE?

PICTURE THIS: It's a gorgeous, sunny day and I'm driving with my darling daughter Kate to buy food for our family Thanksgiving meal. We're going to a store about 10, 15 minutes away because I like it better than the store by us.

We pull into the lot, and I realize I don't have the coupon that will save us 10 percent on groceries.

Got the picture? OK. Now, imagine this: I'm cursing as though the world is coming to an end, fuming over the "wasted" time, and sulking about having to drive all the way back home and then go to the icky store by us.

I am slamming mad—unreasonably, loudly, insanely angry.

Kate, on the other hand, is the model of calm, reminding me that it's a beautiful day, it's not that far, it's no big deal. Suggesting that possibly I need to breathe.

Yeah, well. Instead of breathing, I yank the car into reverse and pull out. And, as we leave the parking lot, we pass:

1. A homeless family holding up a sign asking for help.
2. A woman walking back to her car who is clearly fighting cancer—she's wearing a pink T-shirt and has a pink stocking cap covering her bald head. And, FYI, she's smiling.

"MOM," KATE SAYS,

"I THINK SOMEONE IS SENDING YOU A MESSAGE."

I got the message and I'm sharing it. During this crazy, busy time of year, it's good to remember that we're lucky people. Lucky, lucky people. And it is a wonderful life.

SAVE YOUR LOVE LETTERS.
THROW AWAY YOUR BANK STATEMENTS.

Posted on Jan. 16, 2015

22 ACROSS

Since I'm a writer, you might think I would be great at crosswords. You'd be wrong. I don't know what the capital of Cameroon is, and telling me it's a seven-letter word won't help.

Despite this glaring lack of talent, when my daughter Kate recently started doing crosswords, I happily joined in. And, with some clues, my vocabulary and age have proven useful. For example, Kate wasn't familiar with *Hee Haw*, but I knew the characters might well be called *rubes*.

As we worked our way through one puzzle, I had to ask her to repeat the clues. Frequently. While she graciously repeated and repeated and repeated, I wondered why I was having so much trouble. I finally realized, **I NEED CONTEXT TO UNDERSTAND** whatʼs **BEING SAID.** "What's a three-letter word with cap and pack?" sounds to me like, "What's a three-letter word with ???? and ????." I can tell the vowel involved is an "a" but that's as much as I get.

Cat? Hat? Rat? Where's Dr. Seuss when you need him?

Now, there's a perfectly good reason for this difficulty. I'm half deaf and have been all my life. As I've mentioned before, I typically consider this an advantage: Because I'm half deaf, I pay attention to what people say. I listen carefully to make sure I'm not missing anything. I lip read. I focus.

All these compensation methods are automatic. What I didn't realize —until we started doing the crosswords—is how much I "hear" by context.

For example, "Mom, do you want me to start the dishwasher?" makes perfect sense when Kate says it while she's in the kitchen, after loading the dishwasher. I may actually hear, "Mom, do you ??? me to ??? the dishwasher?" but I know what she means. The context is clear.

There's absolutely no context for 22 across or 60 down.

It matters to me, it matters to Kate, and it matters to you. Context changes everything. **I LOVE YOU** can mean *I want to go to bed with you, you're the best friend anyone ever had, I adore you,* or *I wish to god you would load the dishwasher.*

THAT'S FINE can mean *Okey dokey. That's fine.* Or, it can mean, *I'm exhausted. Please don't ask me to make a decision.*   /171/

And, as we all know, **I DON'T CARE** can mean about 2,000 things, ranging from *Thanks for asking, but it doesn't matter to me* to *If you ask one more time, I'm going to freakin' scream.*

Not that I know that from personal experience or anything.

I don't want to end this on a cross word, so let me gently remind you:

WE ARE ALL PUZZLES.

WE ALL HAVE CONTEXT, HISTORY, SECRETS,

THAT NO ONE ELSE KNOWS.

THE JOY COMES IN FILLING OUT THE BLANKS,

TOGETHER.

P.S. The three-letter word we needed was "ice." I have no idea what the capital of Cameroon is ...

MY FAVORITE DAUGHTER

Looking back over a few of my recent *Creative Instigation* blog posts, I realize I've written more about Mary than about Kate. As a good mom, this makes me twitch—I try to keep things as balanced as possible with the girls.

Although, as Kate will tell you, Mary is the "chosen" one.

I always laugh when she says that, but I'm going to tell you a secret. This is a deep, dark secret no mother ever reveals. By disclosing this confidence, I permanently surrender any claim to the coveted Mother of the Year award. Ah well. Here goes ...

MOTHERS DO HAVE A FAVORITE CHILD.

That's right. All those times when you asked your mom if she had a favorite and she responded, *Of course not, sweetie! I love both/all of you equally!* —well, she was lying. I'm truly sorry to crush your illusions.

Naturally, this revelation brings us to the obvious question: Is Kate, my opinionated firstborn, right? Is Mary, my sweet baby, the chosen child? Is Mary my favorite?

The answer reveals the rest of the secret: **Y E S.** And **N O.**

Mothers do, at times, have a favorite child. But the favorite child changes, sometimes within a minute. Mary strides into the kitchen, grabs her favorite wooden spoon, and bakes up a batch of the best chocolate chip cookies in the world. Favorite child. Kate looks at me with those eagle eyes that miss nothing. Favorite child. Mary asks me to go get sushi with her. Favorite child. Kate invites me to spend Saturday with her, wandering through antique stores. Favorite child.

All things being equal, love isn't. So, I confess. I do have a favorite child.

MINE.

Posted on Sept. 13, 2016

MAKE TODAY SPECIAL

When our daughter Kate turned 17, Tom and I bought her a used VW Passat. Kate's 26 now, a real estate agent with a house of her own. The Passat was old and had over 100,000 miles on it. She wanted something bigger, newer, better.

She went online and found a great deal on an Audi SUV. So, earlier this month, she sold the Passat. A used car transaction—it happens every day. What makes this one special?

The day before she sold her Passat, Kate took it to a car wash and spent about $25 to have the attendants clean it and polish it, inside and out. Then, she drove to a gas station and filled up the tank.

She didn't have to do that. She'd been offered her selling price for the car, sight unseen.

Kate is a mensch*. And the young man who bought her VW? He was thrilled. He didn't have a lot of money. He was buying a 12-year-old car. The polished wheels? The full tank of gas? They mattered to him. They mattered a lot.

**A MENSCH THINKS
ABOUT OTHER PEOPLE
—EVEN STRANGERS—
AND IS WILLING
TO PUT THEIR NEEDS FIRST.**

HOW CAN YOU DO THAT?
WHAT CAN YOU DO,
TODAY,
TO MAKE SOMEONE ELSE
FEEL CARED FOR,
TO MAKE SOMEONE ELSE FEEL SPECIAL?

P.S. There's nothing more satisfying than raising a mensch. Unless it's raising two mensches! Kate and Mary both inspire me to be a better person by their words and their deeds. They make a momma proud.

* *Mensch* is a Yiddish word that essentially means a solid human being, a person of integrity and honor. There are many ways to be a mensch— check out the completely incomplete list on page 92.

Posted on April 14, 2017

SEE THE WONDER

Kate and I recently went on a fabulous mother/daughter vacation to Seattle and Victoria, B.C. Gotta say, it was close to perfect. Even the weather cooperated! At the start of the trip, a friend who lives in Seattle took a day off work to drive us to Snoqualmie Falls. It's gorgeous. After admiring the view from the top, we hiked to the bottom. Along the way, every twist and turn took us to another incredibly beautiful vista—a fairy tale forest, complete with moss-covered trees, soaring in the sunlight.

Kate walked ahead, taking photographs, while I dawdled. And oohed. And ahhed. And repeatedly said, "It's beautiful!"

/176/

After a while of this, our Seattle friend finally asked, "What is?"

"All of this," I said, astonished by the question. "All of it."

He looked around again and quietly said, "You're right. I forget to be amazed."

My friend is a writer, an artist. His world revolves around creativity. It doesn't matter—sooner or later, we all forget to be amazed. This week, don't forget. Open your eyes. See the beauty. Appreciate the wonder.

BE AMAZED.

UPDATE: Mary read the first draft of *Look Up* during a vacation to Portland, and wrote this note in her comments: "On the way to rafting in Oregon, one of the gals we were with asked the guide what that amazing smell was, and the guide looked around and said, 'Oh, that's the trees. I forget because I'm so used to them.' Pretty crazy how we get used to beautiful things and make them ordinary in our minds."

LOOK UP.

May you have purpose.

May you start every day with a healthy mix of gratitude and anticipation.

May you hop out of bed without aches and pains.

May you wake up to good coffee and good people.

May you be somebody's person.

May you forgive and forget.

May you move on.

May you laugh until you cry.

May you cry without shame.

May you enjoy what you eat.

May you remember that everyone needs a little sweets.

May your life be sweet.

May you read good books.

May you play with your toys.

May you look up.

May you make eye contact.

May you listen.

May you be heard.

May you realize it's not all about you.

May you realize that sometimes it is.

May you know, wherever you go,
that you are necessary and appreciated and loved.

MY WISH FOR YOU

MAY YOU LEARN THAT STARTING
AND STOPPING ARE ONE AND THE SAME.

/179/

MAY YOU NEVER BE AFRAID TO STOP.

MAY YOU ALWAYS BE EAGER TO START.

THE ACKNOWLEDGMENTS

Back in 1998, I was watching the Academy Awards when Kim Basinger was named Best Supporting Actress. I remember her going on stage, grabbing the Oscar, holding it up proudly, and proclaiming:

"I WANT TO THANK

EVERYONE

I EVER MET!"

I remember this moment because she was thanking me.

I met Kim Basinger once; I interviewed her when she was a starlet. Did that meeting change her career? Not likely. Would she remember me? Not likely at all. But she and I agree on this: Every step you take gets you where you're going. And everyone you meet along the way matters.

So let me start these acknowledgments by saying, "Thank you, Kim Basinger!" and:

I want to thank everyone I ever met.

Not surprisingly, given my years in journalism and my age, I have met a lot of people. So, out of respect for your time and my memory lapses, I'll keep the formal acknowledgments to a minimum.

There is no better gift for a writer than a reader. This book would not exist without the *Creative Instigation* blog, and the blog would not exist without faithful readers. Special thanks to those of you who have followed my writing over the years, and encouraged me with comments and likes and retweets and smiley faces. Extra big hugs to: Vicki Christensen, Charlotte Cole, Chuck Dymer, CJ Kennedy, and Janee Bovard Lehleitner.

I am grateful to everyone who read the first and second drafts of this book. Thank you for your interest, time, and fabulous feedback— I appreciate you and your input tremendously.

When I'm not writing books or poetry or blog posts, the world's best clients keep me busy with advertising, marketing, and PR copy. Huge thanks to all my clients, with longevity records and complete adoration going out to Karol Hernandez, Kevin Norris, and Stacy Sarris.

My life and my writing have been enriched by a diverse, brilliant, funny group of humans and I'm not even going to try to mention everyone.

You know who you are, and you know that I love you. Please grab a pen, find your alphabetical spot in this woefully incomplete list, and write your name in alongside: Jen Ackerly, Beth Bahner, Sally Beals, Darcie Blake, Michele Boeckholt, Deb Brook, Katie Bulk, Susan Cassaidy, Scott Cole, David Cooper, Angie Davids, Ken DeSieghardt, Katherine Frohoff, Renee Grojean, Katie Huckabee, Michael Johnson, Lucinda Lu, Bill Lyons, Anna Lisa McBride, Tim Murphy, Suze Parker, Steve Popkes, Michelle Smith Puckett, Chris Reaburn, Greg Reid, Sandy Salz, Tyler Shane, Kristie Shay, Pat Stout, Paul Underwood, Bit Vo, Jean Wender, and David Yearout.

My life and my writing have also been enriched by a diverse, brilliant, kind group of humans I've never met: the creative wonders I follow on Twitter and Instagram. Real or fictitious, you make me feel less alone as I sit at my computer, typing away, day after day. Humongous thanks to my IRL friend Bud Simpson for virtually connecting me with Duchess Goldblatt, Peternelle van Arsdale, Jamie Fowler, Pamela Milam, Connie Schultz, Benjamin Dreyer, Charlie Smith, and a host of others. I went with ladies first rather than strict alphabetical order on that list because. The Duchess.

There are times when you look back at life and wonder how you ever got so lucky. That's how I feel when I think about Leslie Adams, Deb Arnswald, Patty Cooper, Ann Egan, Brenda Price, and Cheri Tabel. You have held me up, and held me together. You have applauded me, lifted me, and been there throughout the years. Thank you for you.

SPECIAL THANKS AND ALL MY GRATITUDE:

To Michael and Patricia Snell, literary agents extraordinaire, for faith and confidence in my talents and my ability to persevere. While this isn't the book we worked on together, this one wouldn't exist without you.

To the ever-amazing Amber Lockwood, for showing me—time and time again—what love and courage can accomplish when you're determined to *Look Up*. It's an honor to be your aunt.

To Hedy Goldman, Judy Kass, and Maureen Salz, for friendship that grows stronger with time. They say, "Squirrel!" We say, "Chicken!" Either way, it's good to have peeps.

To Kate O'Neill Rauber and Jody Summers, for all the kind words and gentle pushes. When I was ready to give up, you gave me reason to go on. I doubted. You didn't. You rock.

To Barb Pruitt, for unwavering faith and encouragement. Mom is gone, but you still make me feel like I wrap the silverware better than anyone. For the record, you are also the rare beautiful person who photographs well.

To Deb Hallowell, Linda Penner, and Teena Winter for life-sustaining writers' workshops and many, many white sangrias. You have shaped my writing and blessed my life. We need another trip to Iowa. We need another sangria.

To Vered Harris and Eleanor Harris, for years of love and hugs, and for clapping in delight when I showed you the initial draft of this book. You were the first people to see it and you made me feel like it was on *The New York Times* bestseller list. One of us squealed. (OK, that may have been me.)

To Mark Bonavia, for providing the most articulate, thought-provoking, book-improving insights imaginable as a first reader, and then going above-and-beyond by reviewing the beta version too. *Look Up* would not be what it is without your inspiration and encouragement.

To Mark Levin, for knowing what a writer really needs: an abundance of coffee, conversation, and laughter. You define "hineni" for me—and you can pronounce it correctly. Thank you for always making me feel heard and seen.

To Shanna Haun, for invaluable first reader insights, of course—but for so much more: strength, family, love, friendship. And big thanks to Mackenzie Haun! Having you read the first draft was an unexpected treat.

To Vanessa Bonavia, for—where to begin? This book is what it is because you are who you are. Thank you for being my partner from first idea through first draft, second draft, design, layout, all of it. Mom called me her cheerleader. You are my cheerleader. I'm keeping you.

To Jo Bittel, for bringing this book to life. The cover and text design are the most visible aspects of your impact, but the truth goes beyond that. From our first meeting at the bakery, you became my creative co-conspirator. Fair warning: The book is complete, but you're stuck with me.

To Lynn Dougherty-Underwood, for being my rock. Always and forever. You are my sounding board, my Bobbsey Twin, my conscience, and my *bestfriendinthewholeworldsincefourthgrade*. I could never thank you properly for all that you are and all that you do. You are my person.

To Harry and Eva, for always letting me sit by the window in the back seat of the family car. I was needy. I still am. I can't imagine any siblings I'd rather annoy. But, seriously folks, Mom loved me best. (Fine, fine. She didn't play favorites. Whatever.) I love you both. I love you hugely.

To Kate and Mary, for everything. Grandma used to say she had the best children in the world. This is one of the rare times I disagree with Lillian. You are the best. To say "i carry your heart" is just the start: You *are* my heart. ILYTMAABL.

To Tom, for making it all possible. Thank you for reading the drafts and finding a gentle way to offer spot-on advice on everything from the book title to typos. Thank you for giving me room to grow and time to write. Thank you for all the love and all the laughs and all the years. The longest-lasting fires burn with logs that touch, while leaving space for air.

ABOUT THE AUTHOR

Jan Sokoloff Harness is the mom who greets you at the front door and immediately offers food. Take it. Her brownies are worth every calorie. Jan is the author of the *Creative Instigation* blog and the *Creative Chai* e-book; co-author of *Wackodoodle* with Eleanor Harris; and a contributor to *Healthy Heart and Mind: It's all a Practice* by Shanna Haun. She is also the founder of Sokoloff Harness Communications LLC, an international agency launched in 2002. Her work as a writer, reporter, talk show host, and agency creative director has been honored by groups including the Associated Press, American Women in Radio and TV, the International Association of Business Communicators, the Public Relations Society of America, and The Telly Awards. She is a graduate of the University of Missouri-Columbia School of Journalism and lives in Olathe, Kan., a suburb of her hometown, Kansas City, Mo.

Jan is available for speaking engagements. For more information, please visit creativeinstigation.com or connect on Twitter: @sokoloffharness